PENTAGAMES

Compiled by Pentagram

A Fireside Book
Published by Simon & Schuster Inc.
New York London Toronto Sydney Tokyo Singapore

Fireside
Simon & Schuster Building
Rockefeller Center
1230 Avenue of the Americas
New York, New York 10020

Copyright © 1990 by Pentagram Design Limited

Simultaneously published in Great Britain
by Barrie & Jenkins Limited, Random Century House
20 Vauxhall Bridge Road, London SW1V 2SA

Printed and bound in Spain by Printer Industria Grafica, Barcelona

1   3   5   7   9   10   8   6   4   2

Library of Congress Cataloging in Publication Data
Pentagames / compiled by Pentagram.
p.   cm.
"A Fireside book."
ISBN 0-671-72529-7
1. Indoor games.   2. Puzzles.   I. Pentagram Design.
GV1229.P46   1990   90-33074
793-dc20   CIP

BOMC offers recordings and compact discs, cassettes
and records. For information and catalog write to
BOMR, Camp Hill, PA 17012.

The art of winning is thinking.
It doesn't matter where you are:
you can think, or you can play games.
These games you do both.
With the right skill and wit, you win.

COMMERCIAL
ALPHABET

This is simply a test of your
observation and the power
of advertising and design.

See if you can complete this
picture alphabet using single
letter and pictorial symbols of
well-known organisations,
companies, services or
products. Many trademarks
consist of a mixture of images
but you must stick to single
image designs.

First use a letter symbol,
then a pictorial one. Let's start
with 'A is for apple' (Alitalia/
Apple Computer).

is for

1

TO MAKE A COIN DISAPPEAR

Place a coin at the bottom of a basin of water and ask a spectator to look at it so that his eye, the edge of the basin and the coin are all in line.

While the spectator keeps his eye in the same position, simply remove the water using a syringe or tube.

MATCH WORDS

Arrange the grid of 28 matches. The object of the game is to see how many words can be formed by removing varying numbers of matches. You might find that not many words can be formed by removing less than five or more than 11.

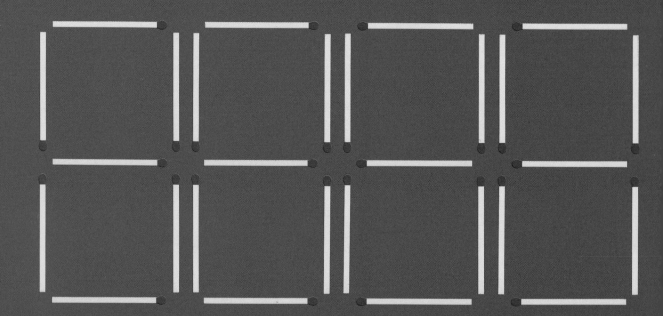

HOPSCOTCH

Stand at the start line and throw a stone into square 1. Hop over 1 into 2 and 3, landing with one foot in either square, hop into 4, jump into 5 and 6 and so on. Turn round at square 10 and go back the same way, picking up your stone in square 1 and jumping over it back to the start. Then throw the stone into square 2 and repeat the sequence, then into square 3 and so on, through to square 10.

In any Hopscotch game, if you touch any of the lines with your feet, put a foot down when hopping, lose your balance or throw the stone out of the square, you must miss a turn and start next time where you left off. You must always jump over any square with a stone on it.

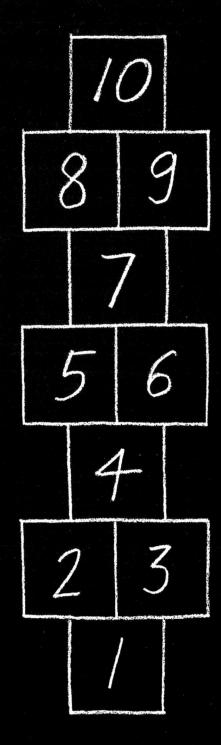

PENTAGRAM

Shuffle a pack of cards. Take the five uppermost cards and place them face down in a horizontal row. Then deal the rest of the pack face down onto these five cards.

Pick up the first pile and look at the bottom card. If it is a 'court' card, any face (picture) card, Ace or 10, replace the pile with that card uppermost. If it is not a court card, remove cards one by one until a court card appears, then replace the pile with this card uppermost. Do the same to the four other piles, looking for court cards of the same suit as the one in the first pile. If any pile does not contain a court card of the same suit, discard it altogether.

Gather up the piles without disturbing the order of the cards and deal the cards again face down, this time into four piles, and proceed as before, looking for the suit that was determined the first time. Repeat the process with three piles and two piles, until there is only one pile left. Once you have found the first court card of that pile, you will have won the game if only the five court cards of the suit remain.

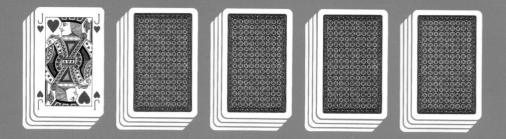

FIVE FIELD KONO

Two players each have seven counters set out on the grid as below. Each player takes it in turn to move one counter diagonally across a square to the next point, either forwards or backwards. Jumping over pieces in the process is not allowed.

The winner is the player who manoeuvres his counters across the board onto the points originally occupied by the opponent.

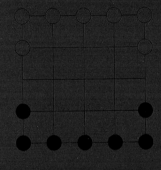

ACHI

Two players each have four counters and take it in turn to place one of them on any vacant point where the lines intersect.

When all eight counters are on the grid, each player in turn moves one of his counters along a line to a vacant point in an attempt to get three in a row. The first player to do so is the winner.

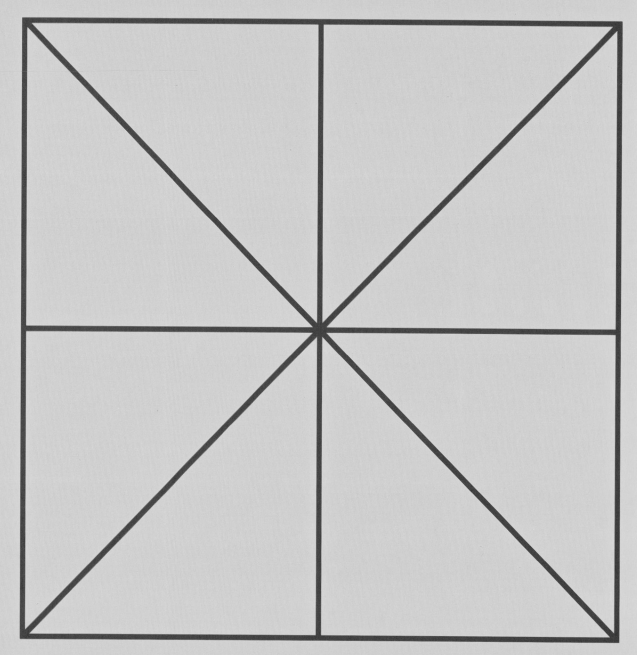

CHECKERS
(DRAUGHTS)

You will need to know the basic rules of Checkers (Draughts) to play other games in this book.

The pieces are set out as below. You can only play on the black squares of the board, and a black piece moves first.

Pieces move diagonally forwards and can only move one square at a time onto an adjacent square. A capture is made by jumping over an enemy piece which is on a diagonally adjacent square and landing on an empty square immediately beyond. More than one piece at a time can be captured in this way.

If a piece reaches the other end of the board, it becomes a King and is 'crowned' by placing an eliminated piece on top of it. Kings can move diagonally backwards and forwards in the same way.

The winner is the player who either captures or blocks all of his opponent's pieces.

TAKE A PIECE OF STRING

This is the basic opening for many of the string games in this book.

Take a piece of string about six feet (two metres) long, shorter for children, and join the ends with a reef knot, shown below.

Insert the thumbs and little fingers into the loop and draw the hands apart. Bring the hands back together, pick up the strings which run across the palms on the index fingers and draw the hands apart.

In all these games, the strings are identified by which fingers they go around. For example, the string which passes around the left hand index finger is the left index loop. The one nearer to you is the 'near' string, and the 'far' string is the one that is further away from you.

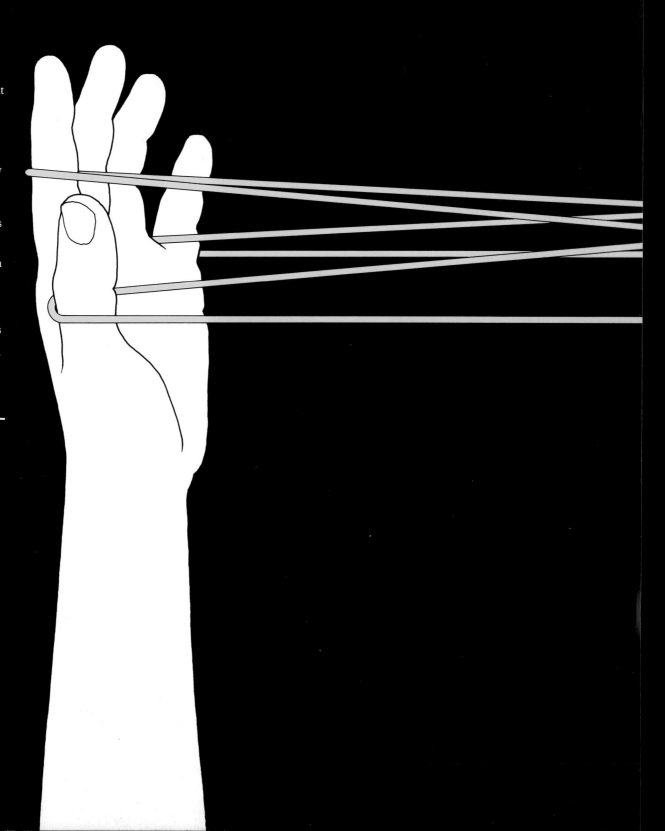

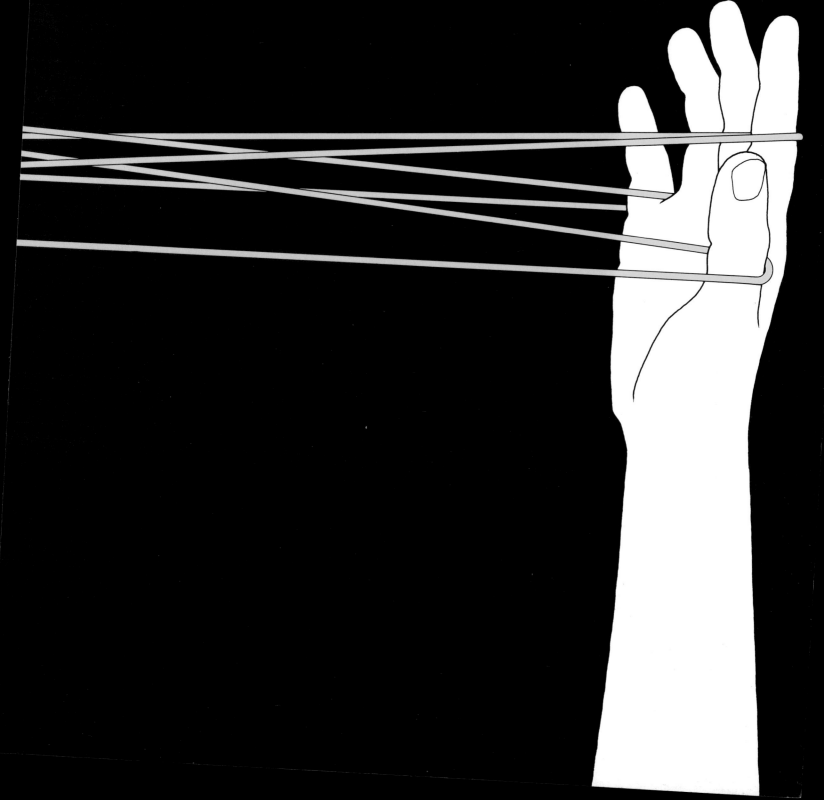

CROSSWORD

On a nine by nine grid, one player writes a word anywhere, across or down, and scores a point for each letter in the word. The other player then writes a word which must connect with the first, and scores a point for each of the new letters.

The players carry on alternately until neither can continue. The points are then added up and the one with the most wins.

VULTURES AND CROWS

One player has one counter as the 'vulture' and the other player has seven counters as the 'crows'. The object of the game is for the vulture to try and kill four crows, or for the crows to trap the vulture.

The first player places a crow on any of the ten points of the board. The second player then places the vulture on another point. A second crow is placed on a third point and then the vulture moves to an adjacent point.

The vulture captures by a short leap over a crow, but cannot capture more than one in any turn of play. The crows are unable to move until all seven have been entered on the board, then a crow can move to an adjacent point at each turn of play.

If the vulture kills four crows, they become too weak to trap it, so it wins the game, and if three or more crows manage to immobilise the vulture they win the game.

11

THE BISHOP

1 Take a standard 30 inch (90 cm) napkin and fold it just below its diagonal.

2 Fold the corners up.

3 Fold the lower section upwards.

4 Take the top layer only and turn it down along the dotted line.

5 Curl the right-hand point backwards.

6 Curl the left-hand point backwards.

7 At the back, insert one point into the pleat in the other point.

8 The napkin stands on a circular base. Pull down the pointed leaves and curl and tuck them inside the plates.

9 A small dinner roll or piece of bread can be placed into the finished design.

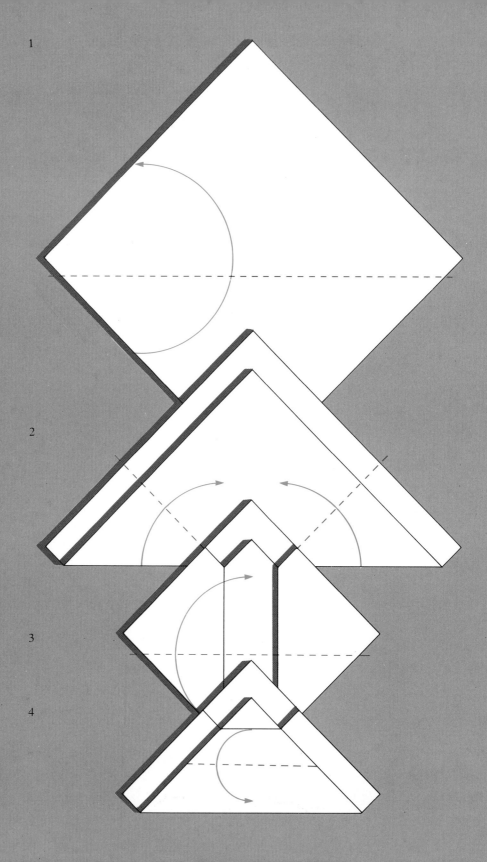

5

6

7

8

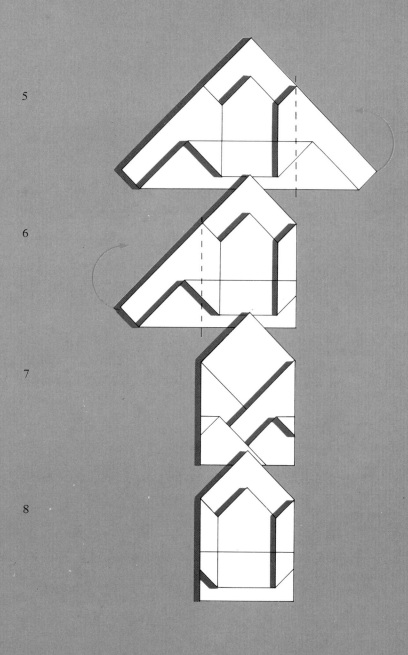

ETERNAL TRIANGLES

Draw a series of dots starting with one in the first row, two in the second, three in the third and so on as far as you want to go.

Two players take it in turns to draw a line connecting any two adjacent dots, the object being to form as many initialled triangles as possible. The game is over when no more triangles can be made. The winner is the player with more triangles than the other.

The game can be made more difficult by scoring extra points for larger triangles that are made of smaller triangles with the same initial, and adding them up at the end of the game.

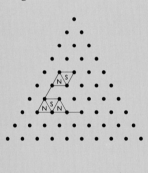

MAGIC FIGURES

Dip the tip of a pencil into water and draw a figure, say a triangle, on a piece of paper.

Fill a basin with water and float the paper, triangle upwards. Then drip water into the triangle to fill it, making sure the water remains within the limits of the lines drawn.

Take a pin, and with its point dipping into the water but not touching the paper, place it at any spot within the triangle. The paper will then begin to move horizontally in a straight line until the geometric centre of the triangle is exactly under the pin point.

Try various shapes and determine the geometric centre beforehand. Wherever you place your pin, watch the paper travel to that centre.

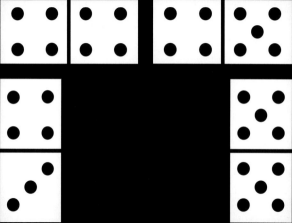

ALQUERQUE

Two players each have 12 counters set out on the grid as below.

Take it in turns to move one counter at a time to any free adjacent point. If an adjacent point is occupied by an enemy counter and the point beyond it free, the enemy can be captured by jumping over and removing it.

When possible, a series of jumps is permitted and a change of direction allowed. If a counter can make a capture it must do so, otherwise it may be removed by the opponent as a bonus before his next turn.

The winner is the player who captures the opponent's 12 counters.

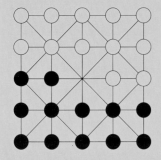

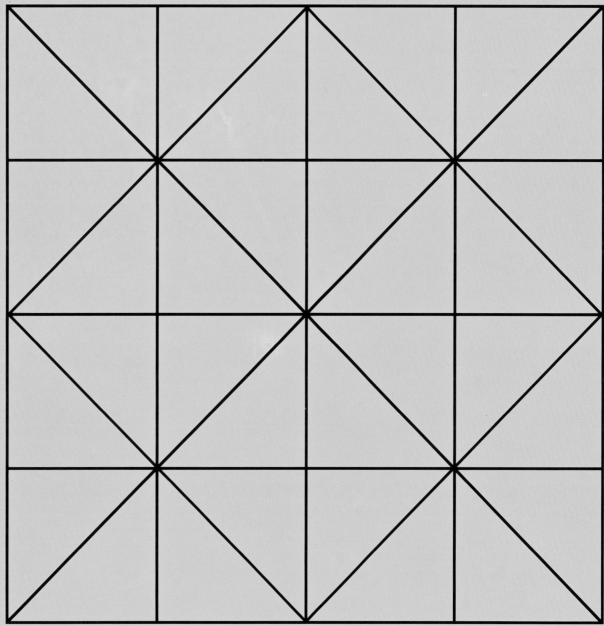

FIVESTONES

This is a series of games
throwing 'stones' into the air
and catching them in various
ways. Each player's objective
is to complete the series of
games first. It is best played
with two or more players,
sitting or squatting on the
floor. You will need a set of
five small cubes or rounded
pebbles.

Each player in turn plays a
game in the sequence or re-
commences with the game he
failed the previous turn. The
games should be played in the
order of complexity in this
book.

Most of the games start
with the same basic throw.
Throw the stones up into the
air from the palm of your
hand and catch as many as
possible on the back of your
hand. Then throw them up
again from the back of your
hand and catch as many as
possible in your palm.

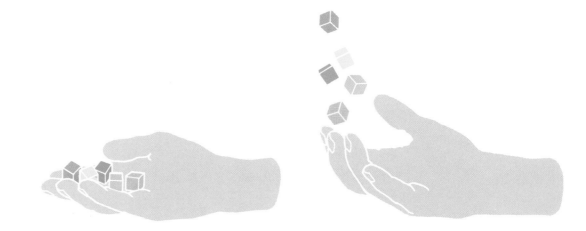

17

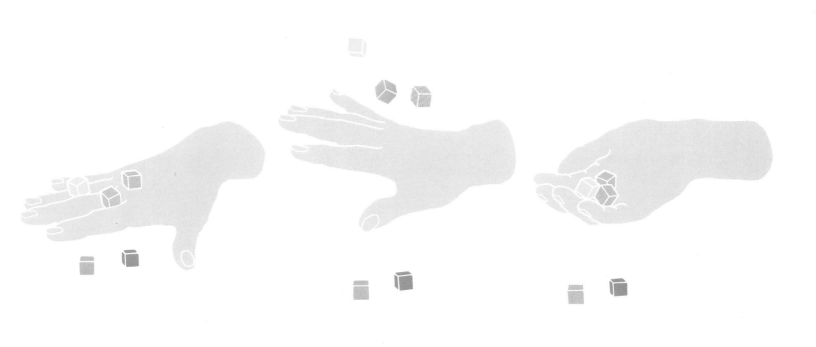

RED AND BLACK

This game is for two players. One player holds a shuffled pack of cards with the backs to his opponent, and then lifts up each card from the front of the pack in turn. The other player has to guess whether the card is red or black, and for each right answer collects the card which otherwise goes to the back of the pack.

Having gone through the whole pack, each player has a pile of cards. The guesser then puts down a card, face up. The other player puts a card beside it and if it matches in value, irrespective of suit, collects all the cards. When one player has all the cards, the game is over.

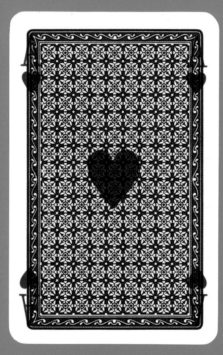 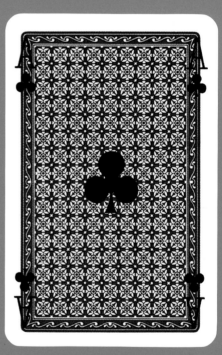

QUADRUPLE ALQUERQUE

Two players each have 40 counters which they set out on the grid as below.

Take it in turns to move one counter at a time to any free adjacent point. If an adjacent point is occupied by an enemy counter and the point beyond it free, the enemy can be captured by jumping over and removing it. When possible, a series of jumps is permitted and a change of direction allowed.

If a counter can make a capture it must do so, otherwise it may be removed by the opponent as a bonus before his next turn.

The winner is the player who captures the opponent's 40 counters.

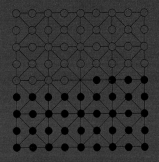

HOLE IN THE HAND

Roll a thin magazine or
newspaper into a tube about
one inch (2.5 cm) in diameter.
Then hold it up to your right
eye, so that you can see all the
way down it.

Bring your left hand up so
that it is just a short distance
away from your left eye, with
your palm facing you and
your little finger resting on the
tube. Close both eyes, then
open them, and you should
be able to see a hole in your
left hand.

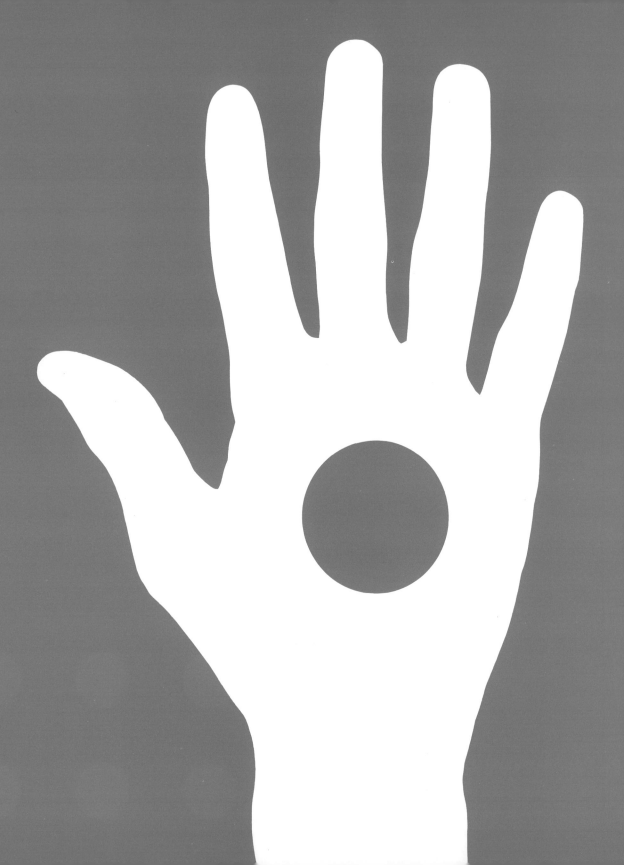

CROWN AND ANCHOR

This is a game for up to seven players. Using card, make three six-sided spinning tops with the aid of the diagram below. Mark the faces of each spinning top with the symbols of the game, and push a nail or cocktail stick through each of the centres.

All players start with an equal number of tokens of any kind, and each player except the banker uses them in turn to place a bet on a chosen symbol. The players place their betting tokens over their symbols, and the banker then spins the tops.

Players may win one, two or three times their stakes from the banker, according to the number of times their chosen symbols appear. Any remaining tokens on the board go to the banker.

Take it in turns to be the banker as he usually wins.

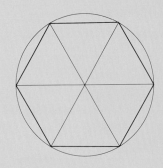

8, but the pieces are set out on the board diagonally.

BANKER

This is a game for two or more players, one of which acts as banker.

All players start with an equal number of tokens of any kind. Each player, except the banker, in turn places a bet on a chosen number on the board. The banker writes down the bet and then throws three dice.

If none of the dice shows the chosen number, the banker wins the bet, and if one die shows the number the player wins the bet. If two dice show the number the player wins twice his bet, and if all three show the number he wins three times his bet. A player may also bet on more than one number.

Any player, including the banker, who loses all his tokens is eliminated from the game. Take it in turns to be the banker as he usually wins.

The pieces are set out as below and each of the 'men' moves differently. Any piece except the King is captured by an enemy piece moving onto its square. White moves first.

Pawns move forward one square at a time, or two squares on their first move. They capture moving diagonally forward one square.

Castles move any number of squares forwards, backwards or sideways. Knights move two squares backwards, forwards or sideways, followed by one square to the left or right of the initial direction moved. They can also jump over pieces in their path.

Bishops move any number of squares diagonally, the Queen can move any number of squares backwards, forwards, sideways or diagonally, and the King can move in any direction, but only one square at a time.

If a King is under attack it is in 'check', and if it cannot escape, it is 'checkmate' and the opponent wins the game. If a player cannot move any of his pieces without putting himself in check, the game is a draw called 'stalemate'.

YOTÉ

This should be played as fast as possible. Two players each have 12 counters, one plays 'pebbles' and the other plays 'sticks'. Each player aims to win all the opponent's counters.

   The player with the pebbles starts by putting one counter in any 'hole'. The other player then places his counter in any other hole. The players then take it in turns to move a counter to any adjacent vacant hole but not diagonally, or to introduce a counter onto the board. A player does not have to place all his counters on the board to play, but must eventually play them all.

   A player wins a counter in an adjacent hole by jumping over and removing it, no diagonal moves allowed. He is then allowed a bonus capture, a choice of removing another of his opponent's counters still on the board.

   It is possible for the game to end in a 'tie' when each player has three counters or less left on the board.

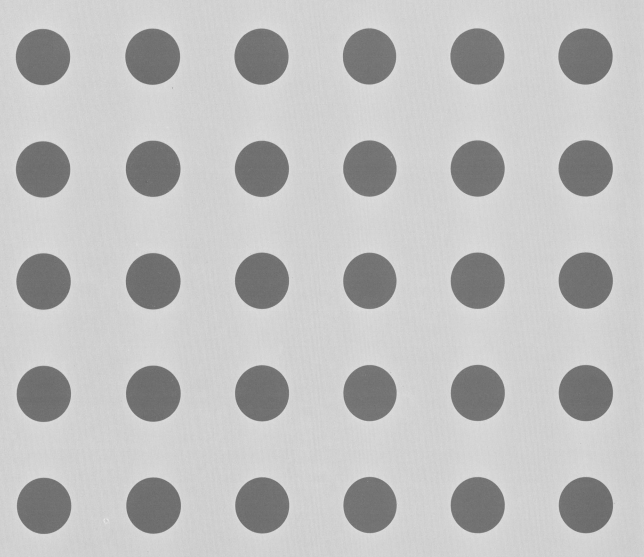

SILHOUETTES

The silhouettes in this book are made by making shapes with your hands and fingers and projecting the shape onto a screen or wall. You will need a good light or lamp behind you to throw a sharp shadow.

If you link your hands in the illustrated way you can make an eagle with outstretched wings. Move your hands to make the bird fly.

SHADOWS ON THE WALL

Place a lighted candle or lamp on a table about three feet (one metre) from a wall or screen, and then a large book between the two.

Place a mirror on the table and cast its reflection on the screen, which will appear as a luminous area once you've found the right angle. You can then project cardboard shapes by moving them between the candle and the mirror.

WORD SQUARES

Start with a four by four grid and try to fill it with a word for each row which reads the same across and down. See how large a grid you can make.

C	R	A	G
R	O	T	A
A	T	O	M
G	A	M	E

NUMBER PLATE BINGO

Each player compiles a bingo card with their own selection of ten two-digit numbers. Players then keep a lookout to find these numbers on the plates of passing vehicles. The first player to complete his card is the winner.

22	24	57	39	26
42	85	58	16	92

SIBERIAN HOUSE

For this you will need to start with the basic opening shown on page 9.

Turn your palms towards you and close your fingers over all the strings except the near thumb string. Flip this string over to the backs of the fingers and return the hands to their normal position.

You now have a loop running round the backs of the fingers. Move both thumbs away from you over the near strings of this loop but under all the other strings. Pick up the far string of this loop on the backs of the thumbs and return.

Lift off the loops from the backs of the hands over the fingers to rest across the other strings. Finally draw the hands apart with the thumbs upwards and you will see the house.

Having built the house, release the index fingers. As the figure is drawn tight the house collapses and you will see two 'Eskimo' men running away.

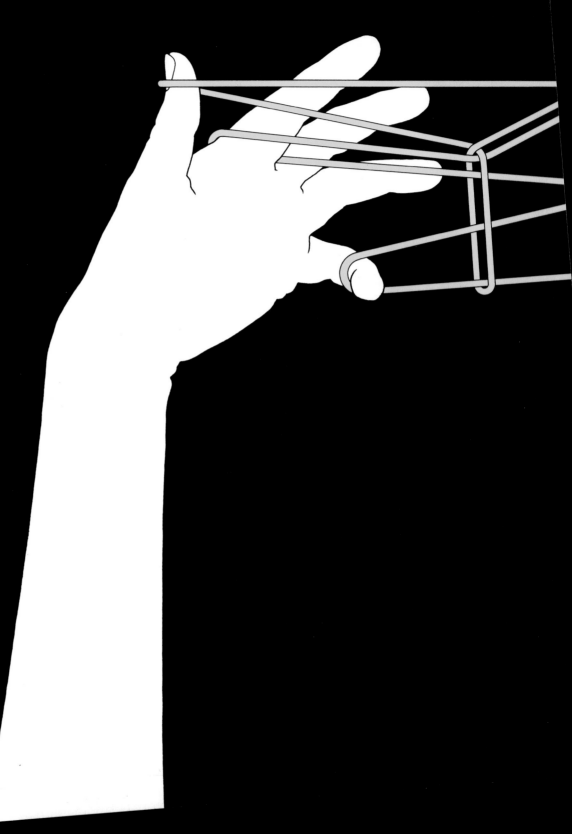

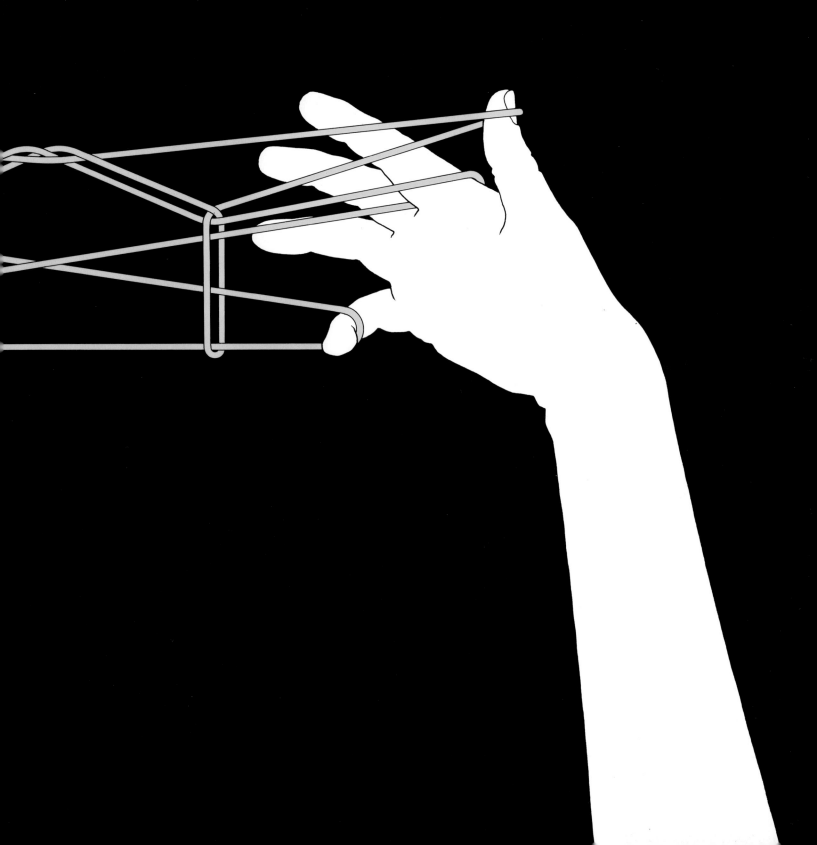

OCTANGLE

Place a counter on any point of the star, and move it along one of the lines to occupy the opposite point. Repeat this in a certain sequence and you should be able to place seven counters on the board with one point left vacant.

If you find this difficult, see the solutions page to see how it's done.

TAC TIX

Lay out 16 matches to make a square. Two players take it in turn to remove any number of matches from any one row or column. The matches taken must be adjacent to each other and have no gaps between them. The winner of the game is the player who forces his opponent to take the last match.

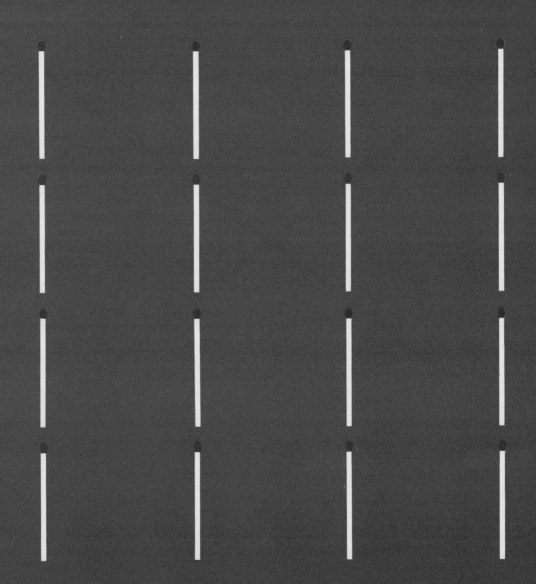

HORSESHOE

Each player starts with two
counters set out as below.
The objective of the game is
to block the opponent so that
he cannot move any of his
counters.
   The first player starts by
moving one of his counters
along a line to the empty point
in the centre. The second
player then moves one of his
counters along a line to the
vacant point.

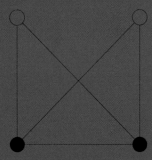

HINKERUDE

Start outside the square, balance on one foot and with the same foot kick a stone into square 1. Then on one foot hop-kick the stone to squares 2, 3 and 4. You can rest on both feet in square 5, then hop-kick the stone to 4 and 6, resting on both feet in 7. Finally, hop-kick the stone to squares 3, 4, 5 and 8, ending on both feet in 9.

If you kick the stone out of any of the squares, or touch any of the lines with either of your feet or with the stone, you are out. The idea is to reach square 9 as quickly as possible.

You can vary the game with your own order of squares, how many hops are allowed in each square and so on.

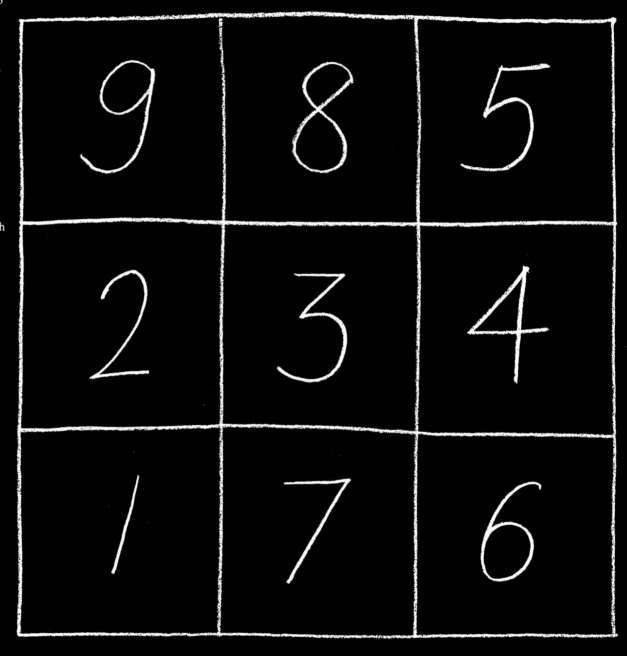

TRAVELLING BINGO

Each player except the 'caller' holds a card with four squares on it. Each square of each card has a different road sign previously drawn by the caller. When any sign appears, the caller names it and any player who might have it on his card crosses it off. The first player to cross out a complete card calls 'bingo' and is the winner.

The game can also be played with other subjects such as animals, makes of cars or filling stations, in fact anything that can be seen at the roadside.

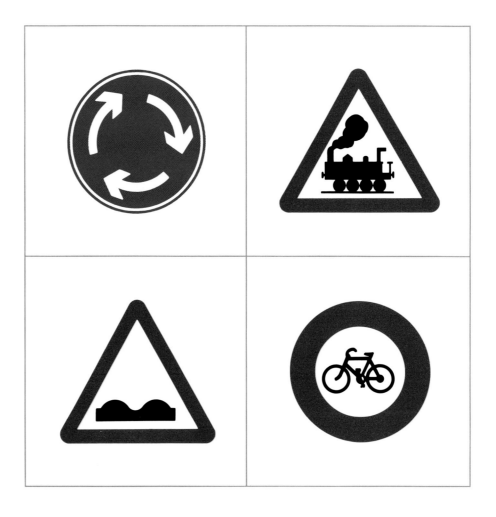

FAN TAN

For this game you will need
a bowl of dried beans and
a stick.
    Any number of players
have an equal number of
tokens of any kind, and elect a
banker who then asks them
to place bets on a number
between one and four. The
banker takes a handful of
beans, puts them in the centre
of the board and with the stick
begins to separate them into
as many groups of four as
possible.
    It is only the beans in the
final group that is important.
This is the number of beans
that the players have bet will
be left, and which determines
whether they win or lose.

36

SLOGANS

As quickly as you can, make up slogans from the letters of passing vehicle plates. Two or more players can score with 10 points for a slogan and 20 if the slogan relates to the shape or any part of the vehicle. This plate on a pink Cadillac could say 'Rock And Roll'.

PAPER AIRPLANE 1

1 Fold a rectangular sheet of paper in half vertically and then open it out.

2 Fold the left edge in to the centre crease.

3 Fold the left folded edge in to the centre crease.

4 Fold the left folded edge in from the centre crease.

5 Score and crease the paper in half horizontally.

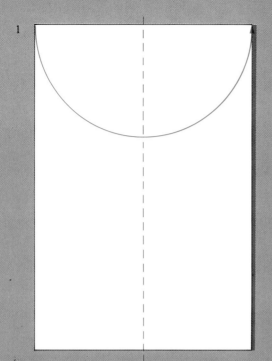

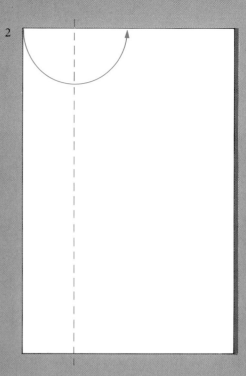

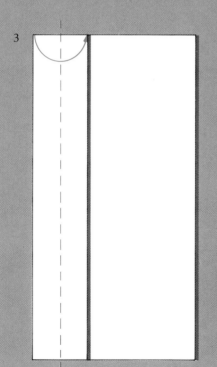

ANIMAL, VEGETABLE, MINERAL

One player thinks of a person, place or thing, but only announces to the other players whether it is an 'animal', 'vegetable' or 'mineral'.

An animal is anything in or made from the animal kingdom, a vegetable is anything from the plant kingdom, and a mineral is just about everything else geological or synthetic.

The other players are allowed 20 questions to find out what it is, but can only be answered 'yes', 'no', 'partly' or 'sometimes'.

The player who discovers the answer is the winner.

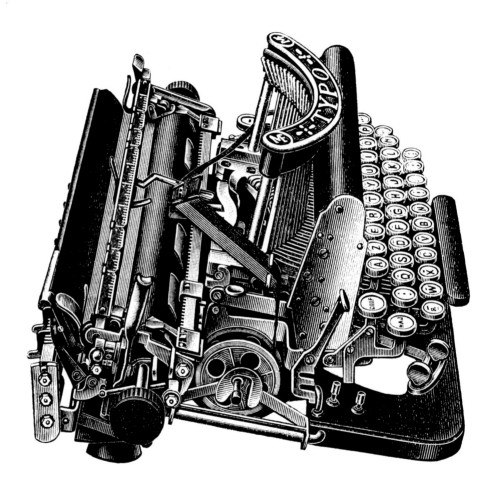

HANGMAN

Think of a word and draw a dash for each letter. The other player then calls out a letter of the alphabet. If the letter features one or more times in your word, write it above the appropriate dash. If it doesn't, start to draw the 'gallows'.

The object of the game is for the second player to guess the word before the gallows is complete and the player is 'hanged'. For the first wrong guess, draw the base of the gallows, for the second draw the upright post and so on, finishing with the man's second leg as below. Secretly write the letter of each incorrect guess as well as adding to the gallows.

Hangman can also be played by both players at once by choosing a word each and taking it in turns to guess each other's. You can also make the game more difficult by deciding on a theme such as films, and using titles or names, or by drawing two parts of the gallows for every incorrect guess.

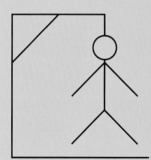

block the wolf so that he cannot move, while the wolf aims to break through them, capturing as he goes, until he reaches the other end of the board. The goats can move diagonally forwards one square at a time, and the wolf can move diagonally forwards or backwards, capturing goats by jumping over them.

WORD PYRAMID

Each player draws a pyramid
of nine rows. The top of
the pyramid is two boxes,
beneath it three boxes, then
four and so on, down to a
base of ten boxes.

   On the word 'go', players
have to fill in the pyramid with
a two-letter word in the top
line, a three-letter word in
the second line, a four-letter
word in the third line and so
on. The first player to fill the
pyramid is the winner.

MAXEY

Draw seven parallel lines about the same length as a match and slightly less than a match-length apart.

Two players start with five matches each, and play one match in turn by placing it onto one of the parallel lines. If two adjacent lines already have matches on them, you can bridge them by playing a match across. You can only bridge a pair of matches once.

Each player scores one point each time he places a match onto a line next to an occupied line, and two points each time he forms a bridge.

When all the matches have been played, the player with the most points is the winner.

THREE MATCHES

Carefully slit one end of a match. Trim the end of another match into a wedge shape and fit it into the slit in the first match. Put both matches on a tablecloth to prevent them slipping and prop them up by leaning a third match against them to form a tripod.

   If you then challenge someone to lift the tripod with a fourth match they will find it impossible.

   All you have to do is insert the fourth match quite low through the point of the tripod, between the two joined matches and the single one. As you do this, push the two joined matches lightly away from the third match until it falls onto the one you are holding. Lower it until the end of the third match passes under the angle formed by the two joined matches. Now raise the match you are holding.

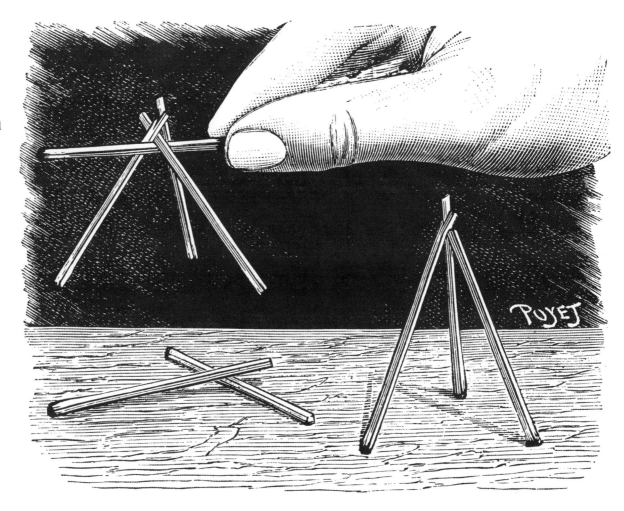

HORSE RACE

This is a game for three or more players using a pack of cards and counters for betting. Each player cuts the pack, and the one with the highest score becomes the banker.

The banker takes the four Aces from the pack and places them as the 'horses' in a vertical row. He then shuffles the cards and deals seven in a horizontal line forming the 'course'. If five or more of these cards are of the same suit, the cards should be reshuffled and dealt again.

Taking into account the course cards, the banker then decides the betting limits of each race, and declares the odds on each horse. If one suit appears predominantly in the course there will be fewer cards of that suit to appear in the race, therefore the banker should choose odds that give him some degree of advantage. The players then state their bets placing their stakes in front of them, and the banker makes a note of how much each player bets on any horse and what the odds are.

To start the race the banker turns over the top card from the deck, and the horse of the same suit is then moved up the course one space. The banker then turns over another card and again moves the horse of the corresponding suit one space. This continues until the winning horse passes the winning line.

The banker then collects all bets placed on the losing horses, and pays at the quoted odds each bet on the winning horse.

WARI

The 'board' for this game is two rows of six holes, but you can use cups and saucers.

Both players sit on either side of the board, the six holes nearest each player forming his row. Four counters as 'seeds' are placed in each hole to open the game.

The first player picks up the four seeds in any of his holes and 'sows' them one by one in an anti-clockwise direction in the next four holes. The other player then does the same with four seeds from one of his holes. The players take it in turns to sow all the seeds from any of the holes in his row.

If in a player's turn the last seed to be sown goes into one of his opponent's holes and that hole contains either two or three seeds, he wins the seeds and removes them from the board. He also wins the seeds in any adjacent holes that contain either two or three seeds.

Once a hole contains 12 or more seeds, a sowing from that hole will take more than one complete circuit of the board. When this happens, the original hole is left empty and stays empty for the rest of the game. The player who still has seeds in his holes when the opponent has none is the winner.

If seeds are being moved with neither player gaining anything, the game can be closed. Each player then takes the seeds from his own row and adds them to the seeds he has won. The player with the most is the overall winner.

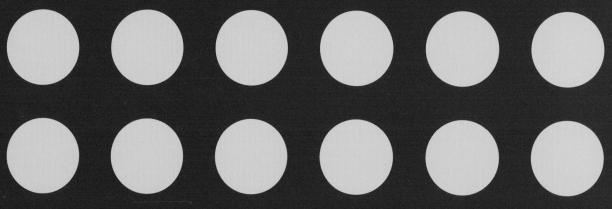

PENNY FOOTBALL

One player, the 'attacker', sits at the end of a table and arranges three coins in a triangle. The other player, the 'defender', sits at the opposite end with one hand on the table closed so that only the index and little finger stick out and rest on it. Between the fingers is the 'goal'.

The attacker 'kicks off' by flicking one of the coins to break the triangle. He must then try to flick a coin into the defender's goal.

Although the attacker can take as many turns as necessary, any coin he kicks must go in a path between the other two coins and not touch either of them. The coin must also hit the defender's knuckles on the table in order to score a goal. If the attacker breaks one of the rules or loses a coin off the table, the players exchange roles and start a new game.

Agree on a time limit for each game and number of official times each player should be the attacker. When you have added up the game scores, the player with the most goals is the winner.

TRAVELLING ALPHABET

See if in sequence you can collect the complete alphabet by spotting things that begin with each letter. If you spot an airfield for A you must spot something for B before you go on to C. When you come to X use objects beginning with 'Ex' instead. Speed the game up using initial letters from road signs or advertisements.

BRIDGE THE WORD

Draw seven lines across a
piece of paper. Then choose a
six-letter word and write it in a
column on the left-hand side,
and in the reverse order on the
right-hand side. The game is a
race to see who can 'bridge the
word' most successfully.

Each player in turn writes a
word starting with a left letter
and ending with its corresponding right letter, as below.
The player with the longest
word is the winner.

```
P                       L
E                       I
N                       C
COMMUNICATION
I                       E
L                       P
```

CARD DOMINOES

Deal a pack of cards face down in a clockwise direction for two or more players. Each player then sorts his hand of cards into suits and sequence.

The player with the seven of diamonds starts the game by putting it face up in the centre. The other player, or the player to his left, must then put down the eight or six of diamonds above or below it, or another seven next to it. If this is not possible, he declares a 'pass' and play then goes back to the first player or to the next player on the left.

Each player in turn adds a card to a sequence, starts a new sequence with a seven, or passes. The four sequences are built from the seven upwards to the King, and downwards to the Ace.

The first player to have put down all his cards is the winner.

MORA

Two players sit face to face with their fists closed. Simultaneously, they each extend one or two fingers while at the same time calling 'one' or 'two'.

The number you call out is the number of fingers you guess your opponent will show. If you both guess correctly, or if you are both wrong, no-one wins. If one player guesses correctly, then he is the winner. If you play with tokens of any kind, the number of tokens you can win in a single call is the total number of fingers shown by both players.

The game can also be played in the more complex version. Each player shows and calls either one, two or three.

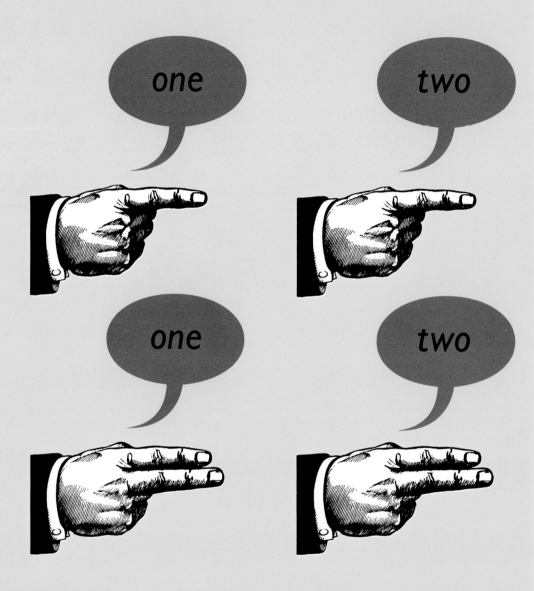

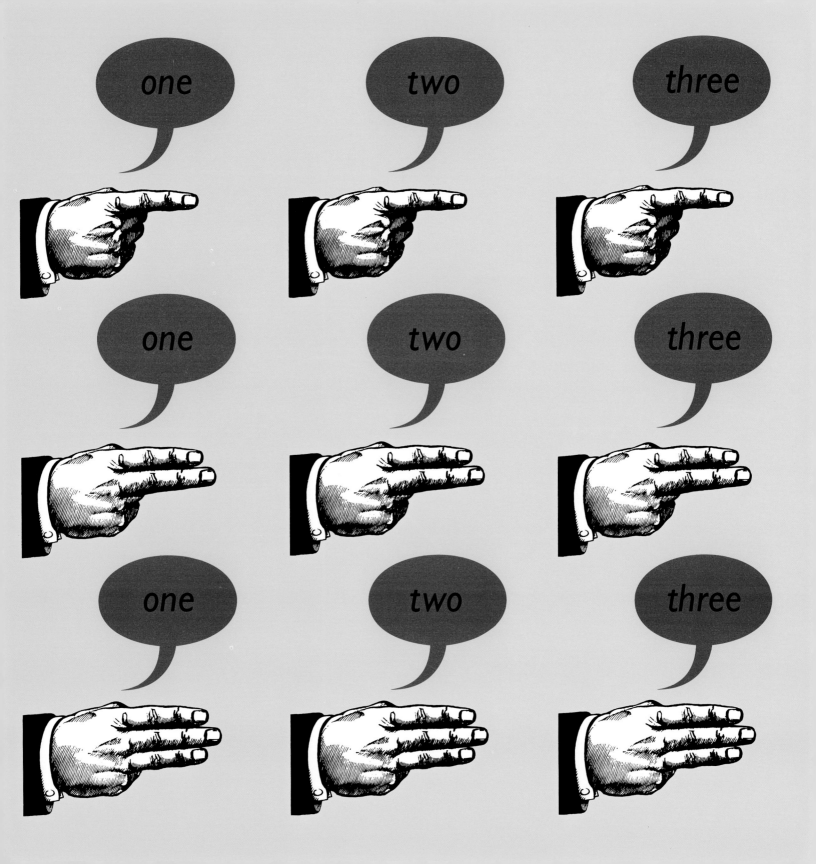

MU TORERE

Each player has four counters set out as below, and takes it in turns to prevent the enemy counters from moving.

There are three types of move. A counter may be moved from an arm to the centre – providing that one or both of the adjacent arms are occupied by an enemy, from one of the arms to an adjacent arm, and from the centre to an arm.

You can vary the game by restricting the movement of a counter from the arms to the centre only for the first two moves of each player. Only one counter is allowed on any point and jumping is not allowed.

The player who succeeds in immobilising the opponent is the winner.

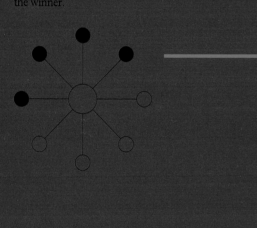

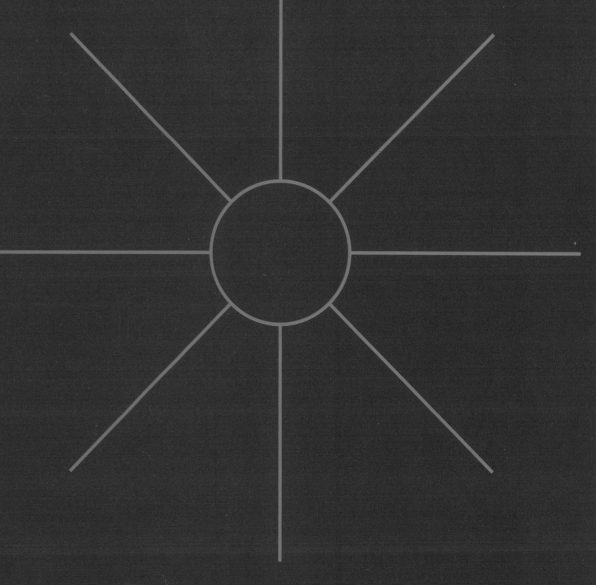

THE WINDMILL

Using two packs of cards, pick out four Kings, one from each suit, and one Ace. Then place the Ace with the Kings diagonally around it. Shuffle the remaining cards, and turn over the first eight to complete the windmill.

The object of the game is to build upon each of the Kings a single descending sequence from King to Ace, and upon the central Ace, four distinct ascending sequences, in no particular suit order, from Ace to King.

First look at the eight 'sail' cards surrounding the Ace and Kings to see if any of them can be played, either in ascending order to the Ace or in descending order to a King. Move them accordingly and fill up any gaps with cards from the pack, then deal from the pack to a separate pile, playing any cards that you can in the process. If one of the sail cards is playable to the Ace or to a King, preference is given to the Ace.

To win, the centre should have four sequences with a King on top, and four separate piles with an Ace on top when all the cards have been dealt.

SCISSORS, PAPER, STONE

This quick game can also be a good way of deciding who goes first when starting any other game.

Two or three players hide one hand behind their backs, and on the count of three bring out the hand as 'scissors', 'paper' or 'stone'. Scissors score over paper because they can cut it, paper scores over stone because it can wrap it, and stone scores over scissors because it can blunt them. The winner of the round scores a point.

If three people are playing and all three show a different sign, no-one scores because the signs cancel each other out. If, for instance, two players show stone and one scissors, both of the stones get a point. If two players show paper and one scissors, then the scissors score two points.

A TRIO OF
CHAMPAGNE GLASSES

Holding a thin wooden rod,
try various positions until you
can support a tall champagne
glass on the other end in a
horizontal position.

 With your other hand, hold
the foot of a second glass on
a table, place your end of
the rod into it and find the
position where the horizontal
glass is supported.

 When you repeat the
procedure with another glass,
the combination will support
itself.

MAN IN THE MOON

Each player has 12 coins, one playing 'heads' and the other 'tails'. The objective is to reduce the opponent's 'men' on the board to only one 'Man in the Moon'.

The players take it in turn to place a 'man' on any square except the centre one. When all the men are down, the first player moves one of them to the centre square. The players then take it in turns aiming to capture the opponent's men, by moving one piece at a time in any direction except diagonally.

A player may capture any opponent's man which falls between two of his own. More than one man can be captured in this way as long as there are no intervening spaces. A capture can only be made by a moving player after all the men are on the board and the first move has been made. If a player cannot move, the other player must continue until the other can.

The winner is the player who succeeds in making his opponent the 'Man in the Moon'.

TANGRAM

Make a tangram set with the
aid of the diagram below using
card or wood. The best size
is a four by four inch (10 cm)
square. Lightly mark the
guidelines and then carefully
cut out the set which will
comprise five triangles, one
rhomboid and one square.

The game is to produce a
silhouette using all seven 'tans'
without any overlapping.
Compete with someone else
to see how many shapes you
can make in a set time limit, or
experiment and make your
own designs. Copy the ones
illustrated to get you started.
Well over 1000 shapes can be
made, including human
figures, animals, buildings
and alphabets.

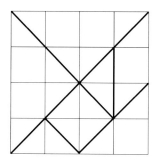

SPELLING BY NUMBERS

Tap all the numbers into a calculator and then turn it upside-down to read the 'letter' that each one makes. The game is putting numbers together to make words.

Challenge other players to see how many words can be made in a set time limit, or try to make phrases and have a conversation. The game can give you a vocabulary of over 50 English words.

hELLO

SPOOF

This is a game of bluff. The aim is to guess the total number of objects hidden in the hands of all players.

Three or more players each have three objects, such as coins, matches or paperclips, and conceal any number of them in their fists behind their backs. On the count of three all the players hold out their fists, and each player in turn, in a clockwise direction, has to guess the total number of objects concealed. Each guess must be different.

Everyone opens their fists and the objects are counted. The player who guessed correctly or nearest the number, wins the round.

PRESSMAN'S HAT

1 Take a large sheet of newspaper and fold it once.

2 Fold the top sheet of the unfolded edge to the edge of the triangle, and repeat this to form a cuff. Then turn it over.

3 Fold the sides of the triangle in to meet the centre crease.

4 Fold the bottom corners up to meet the cuff.

5 Fold the bottom of the paper up to meet the cuff and unfold. Fold the whole flap up and tuck it into the cuff. Turn it over from top to bottom.

6 Fold the peak of the triangle and tuck it into the cuff to make a rectangle.

7 Open the hat wide and two 'ears' will stick out of the top and bottom. Fold the ears and tuck them into the cuffs. Then square the hat, creasing the corners.

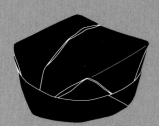

1

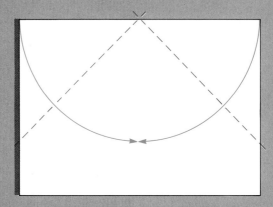

2

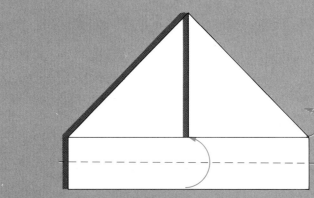

3

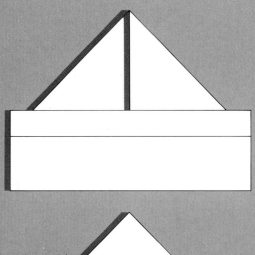

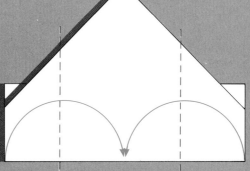

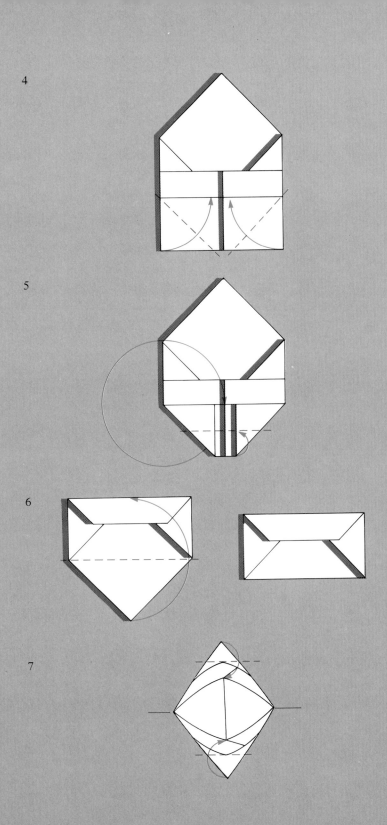

BOXES

Using squared or plain paper, mark out ten rows of ten dots. Two players take it in turns to draw a straight line connecting any two adjacent dots, either horizontally or vertically.

The object of the game is to make the fourth line of any square and claim it, marking it with your initial as below. When all the dots have been joined, the player with the most boxes is the winner.

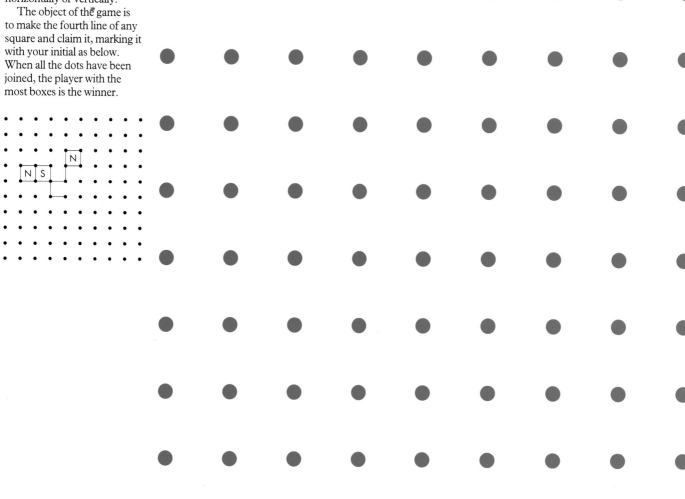

From a line about six feet (two metres) from the square, shoot a marble at the targets and win any that you knock out of the square. If your 'shooter' comes to rest within a hand's span of one of the targets, you can also win this marble. If you cannot reach a target marble, your shooter stays where it is and becomes another target.

See how many shots it takes you to clear the square.

SPIN A PLATE ON A NEEDLE

Split two corks down the middle, and push the prongs of four table forks into each of the four halves at right angles to the flat, cut surface.

Place the four corks around a plate, making sure that the prongs of the forks are touching the edge of the plate.

By careful manipulation you should be able to set the plate spinning on the point of a needle pushed head downwards into the cork of the bottle. The rotary movement should continue for some time.

THE COTILLON

Pick out all the fives and sixes from two packs of cards. Arrange them in a circle in pairs of the same suit, with the six on the right of the five each time, and so that a pair of black cards is next to a pair of red. Then shuffle the remaining cards.

Turning over a card at a time, if you reveal a card of the same suit and of ascending order to any of the sixes, place it on the corresponding six. If you reveal a card of the same suit and of descending order to any of the fives, place it on the corresponding five. For example, on the six of hearts place the seven of hearts up to the Queen, and on the five place the four down to the Ace and King. If you cannot play a card, put it face down into a 'waste heap' in the centre of the circle.

To win you must end up with all the right-hand heaps crowned with a King and all the left-hand heaps with a Queen. You can also deal through the waste heap twice if you come to a standstill.

MAN IN BED

For this you will need to start with the basic opening shown on page 9.

Pick up the near little finger strings on the thumbs by moving the thumbs away from you under the index loops, up into the little finger loops, and returning under the index loops.

Pick up the far thumb strings on the little fingers by passing the little fingers towards you over the far index strings, under the near index string, up into the thumb loop and returning.

Finally release the index fingers and draw the figure tight, representing a man lying on a bed. Release the little fingers and the bed breaks.

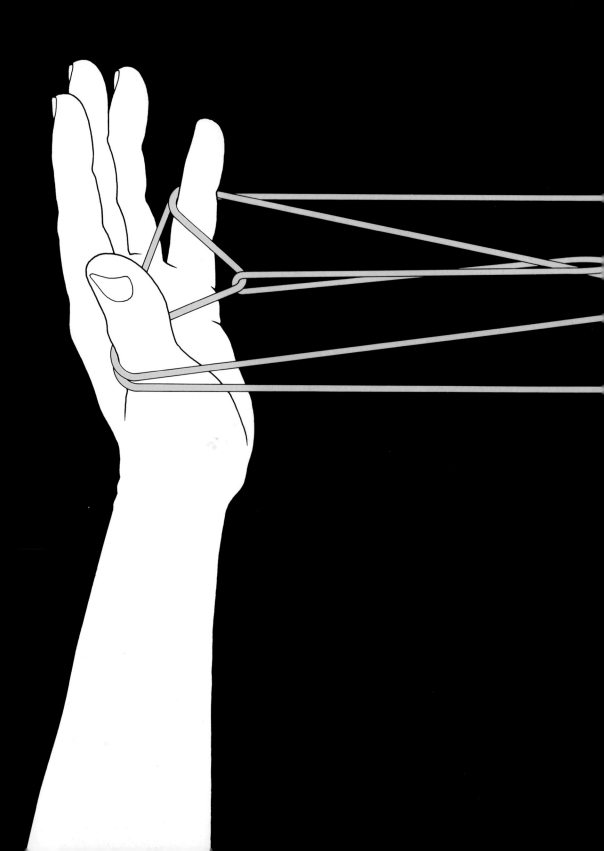

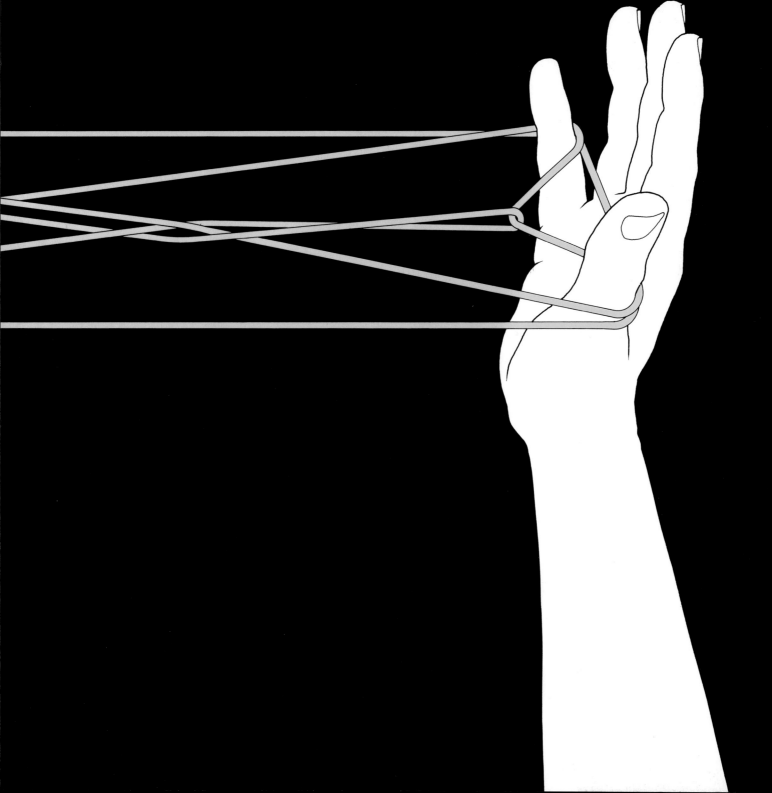

TRICKY THREE

Place three banknotes on a table side by side, one of them face up, and two face down. Ask your opponent to turn over two notes at a time, and try and get them all face down in three moves.

The secret is in the starting position for when you do it. See the solutions page.

MAKE AN ELEPHANT

Give everyone a sheet of
newspaper, then turn out the
lights and ask them to tear out
an elephant. When the lights
are turned on, the player with
the shape that most resembles
that of an elephant is the
winner.

PAPER AIRPLANE 2

1 Fold a rectangular sheet of paper in half vertically and then open it out.

2 Turn the paper over, then fold the top right corner down, slightly overlapping the centre crease.

3 Fold the top left corner down slightly overlapping the centre crease.

4 Turn the paper over and fold the flap over the triangle.

5 Fold the top point down.

6 Double fold the centre and the wing tips.

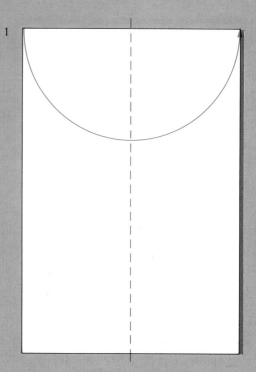

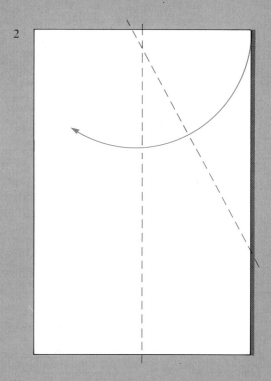

3

4

5

6

LIFT FIFTEEN MATCHES WITH ONE

Lay a match on a table and link 14 matches head up across it. Then place another match across the top of the 14 linked ones. By picking up the first match, you will be able to lift all 15 matches.

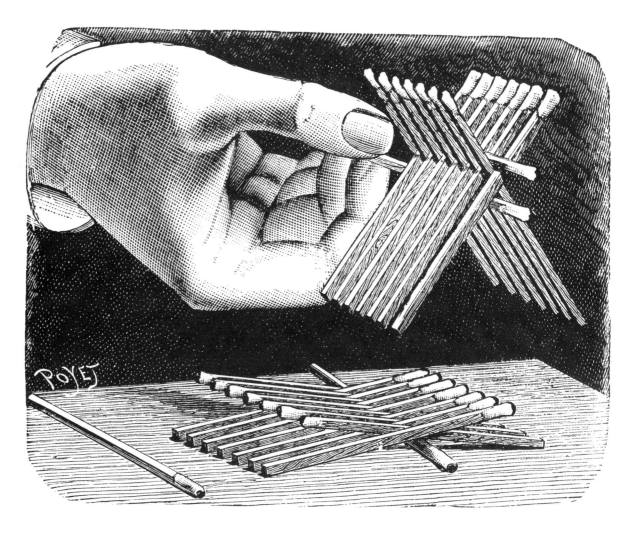

FIVESTONES
ONES, TWOS, THREES, FOURS

These four games follow the same principle and are played as individual games within the sequence of Fivestones. For each of these games, first perform the basic throw on page 17. Start your sequence of Fivestones games with 'Ones' unless you caught all the stones in the basic throw, when you can start with 'Twos'.

'Ones' is played by scattering all five stones from your hand onto the floor. Pick up one stone and throw it in the air. Before catching the stone that's up in the air, pick up one of the stones from the floor with the same hand. Transfer the stone you pick up to your other hand and continue until all the stones have been picked up.

'Twos' is played in the same way as Ones, except that you pick up two of the stones from the floor in your throwing hand. Transfer the two stones you pick up to your other hand then pick up the remaining two stones in the same way. 'Threes' and 'Fours' are played in the same way.

When you have completed this first series through to 'Fours', you can next play 'Pecks' on page 94.

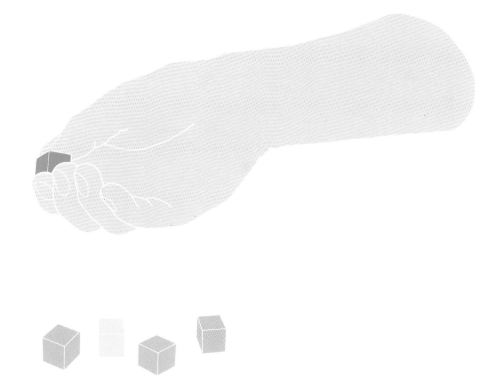

THE STAR

Shuffle and cut a 'piquet' pack of cards, a standard 52-card pack from which the twos, threes, fours, fives and sixes have been removed.

Turn over and place four cards in the form of a cross, and the next four cards at angles between them. Then place another card on the end of each of these eight, to make sixteen cards in the shape of a star. Place the remaining sixteen cards in the centre of the star to form the 'stock'.

Turn up the top card of the stock, and if it corresponds in value, irrespective of suit, to one of the cards of the star, remove it together with its pair. Turn up the next card of the stock and continue in the same way until all the cards of the stock and the star have been paired and put aside.

When you remove one of the cards adjacent to the stock, replace it with its own adjacent card, so that the 'inner circle' is kept complete. If none of the cards of the star will pair with the top card of the stock, place the card in one of the vacant spaces of the 'outer circle'.

If you cannot pair the top card of the stock with one in the star, and the outer circle has no vacant spaces, then you have lost. If you exhaust all the cards in the stock and there are only duplicate cards remaining in the star, then remove them in pairs to win.

73

PERALIKATUMA

Two players each have 23 counters which are set out on the grid as below.

Take it in turns to move one counter at a time to any free adjacent point. If an adjacent point is occupied by an enemy counter and the point beyond it free, the enemy can be captured by jumping over and removing it. When possible, a series of jumps is permitted and a change of direction allowed.

If a counter can make a capture it must do so, otherwise it may be removed by the opponent as a bonus before his next turn.

The winner is the player who captures the opponent's 23 counters.

WOOD CARRIER

For this you will need to start
with the basic opening shown
on page 9.

Transfer the little finger
loops to the thumbs and index
fingers by passing the thumbs
and the index fingers over
the index loops and up into
the little finger loops. Release
the little fingers. Each hand
now has an index finger loop
and a thumb loop and, nearer
the tips, a combined index/
thumb loop.

Lift off the thumb loops
over the index/thumb loop,
and curl both thumbs away
from you and down into the
thumb loop which you have
just released. The index/
thumb loops will slide from
the thumbs.

With the thumbs pointing
downwards and the palms
facing away from you, draw
the figure tight. The two
middle strings represent a
headband used for carrying
wood, the other strings the
wood itself.

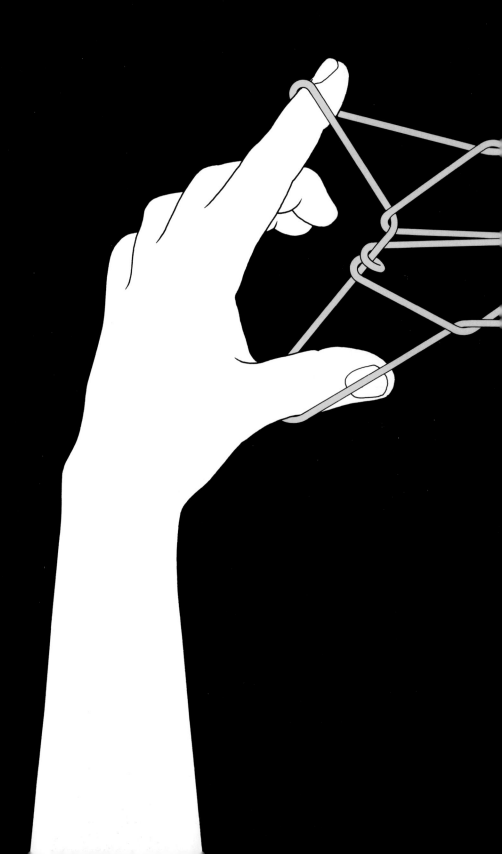

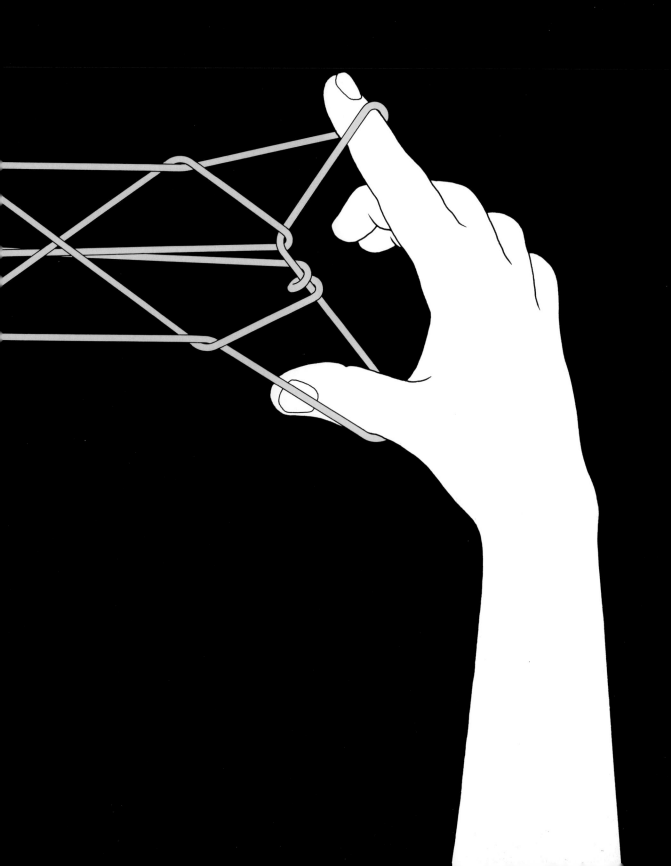

MONDAY-TUESDAY HOPSCOTCH

Stand in 'Earth' and throw a stone to 'Monday'. Hop over Monday into 'Tuesday', then 'Wednesday' and so on to 'Sunday'. Rest in Sunday then hop back to Tuesday. Pick up the stone, hop over Monday again and back to Earth. Repeat this sequence for every day of the week, each time hopping over the square with the stone in it.

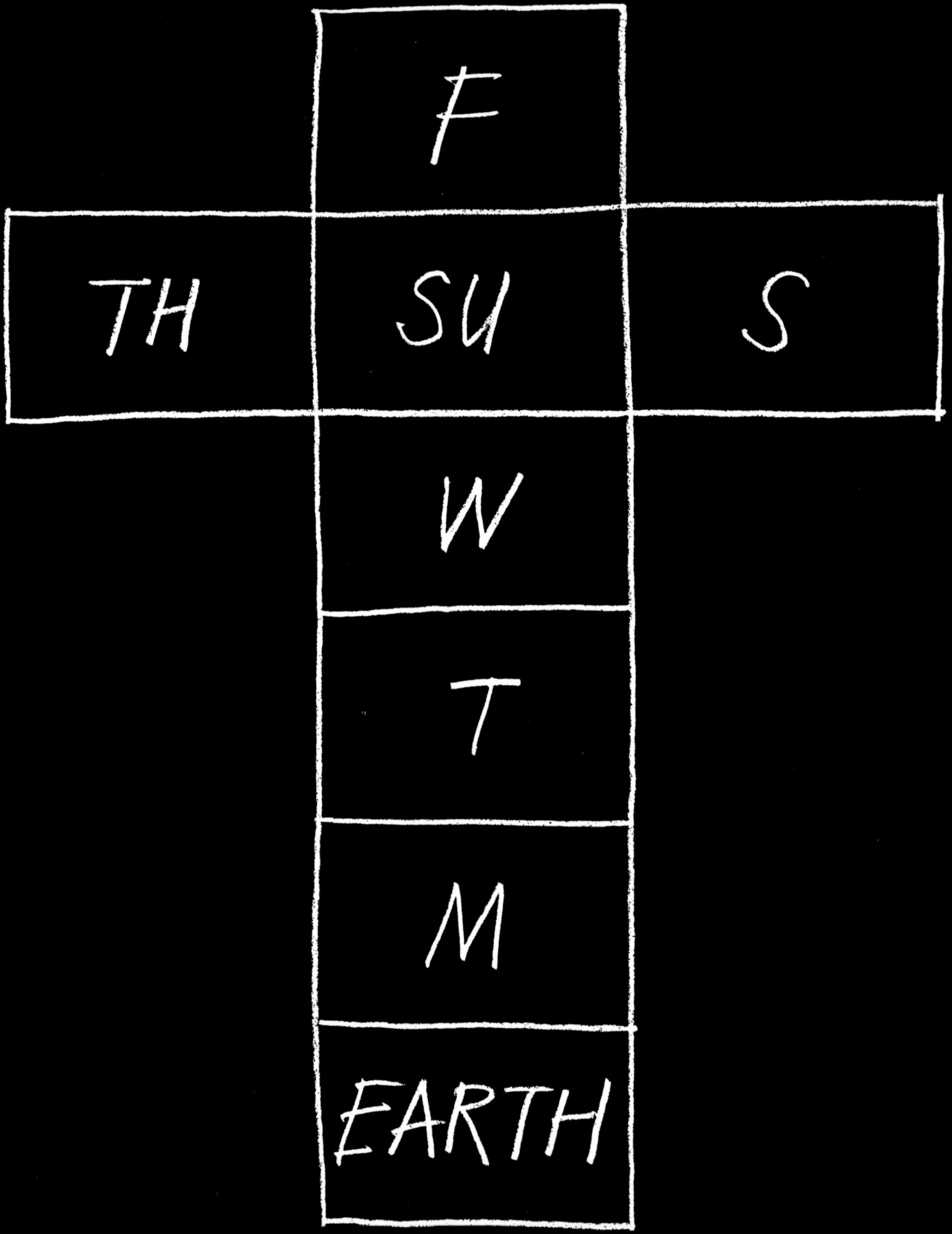

F

TH | SU | S

W

T

M

EARTH

GLUCKSHAUS

For this game you need two dice and a number of counters for two or more players. The aim is to win as many counters as possible.

Each player starts with an equal number of counters and takes it in turn to throw the dice to enter 'the house'. If the dice total corresponds with any of the 'room' numbers, the player places one counter in that square. If there already is a counter in the square the player takes it but stays where he is. A player cannot enter the house with a total throw of 4, and so passes the dice to the next player.

If the dice throw totals 7, the player puts a counter in the 'wedding room', but cannot pick up any counters which may already be in it. A throw of 2 is the 'lucky pig's room' when the player can take every counter off the board except the wedding one. A throw of 12 is the 'king's room' when the player can collect all the counters from the board.

Players are out of the game when they run out of counters, and the winner is the last player left.

Vary the game playing with tokens of any kind, and put down a number of tokens corresponding with the number in that square, with the exception of the 12 and 3.

	12	
11	7	3
	10	
6	9	5
	8	
	3	

PENTALPHA

The object of the game is to
introduce nine counters or
coins onto the board in a
certain order.

Place the first counter on
any point of the board, calling
'one'. Then move it in a
straight line to another point,
calling 'two', and on to a third
point, calling 'three'. Now
repeat this one-two-three
sequence with each of the
counters. Each time, the first
and third points must be
empty but the second point
can be occupied.

one sideways in any direction.

With practice you should be able to complete the game within 50 moves but it is almost impossible to do it in less than 45.

THE MITRE

1 Take a standard 30 inch (90 cm) napkin and fold it into three.

2 Fold the edges to the centre.

3 Fold two corners to the centre line.

4 Holding the napkin at the edges marked with red dots, fold it backwards along the red dotted line allowing all the corners to stand up.

5 Tuck the left-hand point inside the pleat.

6 Tuck the other point into the pleat on the reverse side.

7 The napkin stands on a circular base.

8 A small dinner roll or piece of bread can be placed into the finished design.

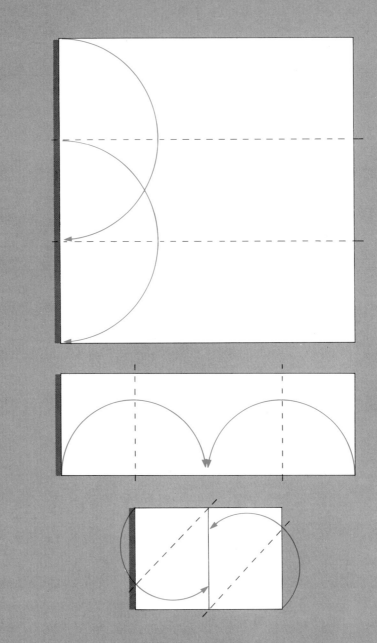

4

5

6

7

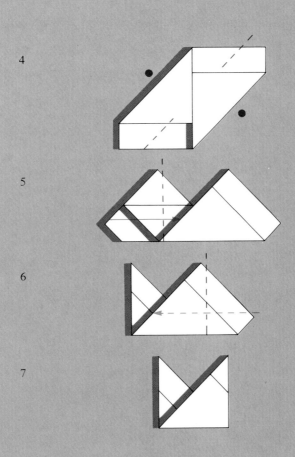

QUADRILLE

Pick out all the Queens, fives and sixes from a pack of cards. Arrange the Queens so that the two reds are vertical and the two blacks horizontal, making a square space between them. Then arrange the sixes at right angles to their corresponding Queens, and follow with the four fives placed diagonally adjacent to their corresponding Queens.

Turning over a card at a time from the pack, if you reveal a card of the same suit and of ascending order to any of the sixes, place it on the corresponding six. If you reveal a card of the same suit and of descending order to any of the fives, place it on the corresponding five.

On the six of hearts place the seven of hearts up to the Jack, and on the five place the four down to the Ace and King. If you cannot play a card, put it face down into a separate 'waste heap'.

If you proceed as above until the Kings and Jacks lie beside their respective Queens, you have won. You are allowed to deal three times from the waste heap if you don't place all the cards the first time.

PUT AND TAKE

Using card, make an eight-sided top with the aid of the diagram below. Mark each of the faces and then push a nail or cocktail stick through the centre for it to spin.

Each player puts an agreed number of tokens of any kind into the pot. Players then take it in turns to spin the top and put into or take the indicated amount from the pot. 'Put All' indicates that a sum equal to the amount already there should be put into the pot, and 'Take All' indicates that the entire contents of the pot should be taken.

The winner is the player left when the others have lost all their tokens.

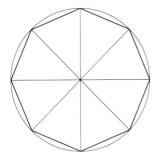

NINE MEN'S MORRIS

Two players each have nine counters or 'men' and take it in turns to place one of them on any vacant point where the lines intersect. Each player's objective is to get three men in a row along any line forming a 'mill' and to prevent the opponent from doing so.

When all men are on the grid the players take it in turns to move one of them along a line to any adjacent vacant point in an attempt to form further mills. Every time a player makes a mill he can remove one of the opponent's men that is not part of a mill unless no others are available.

The game is won when the opponent is left with only two men or when one player is immobilised.

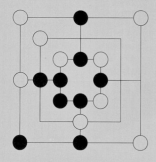

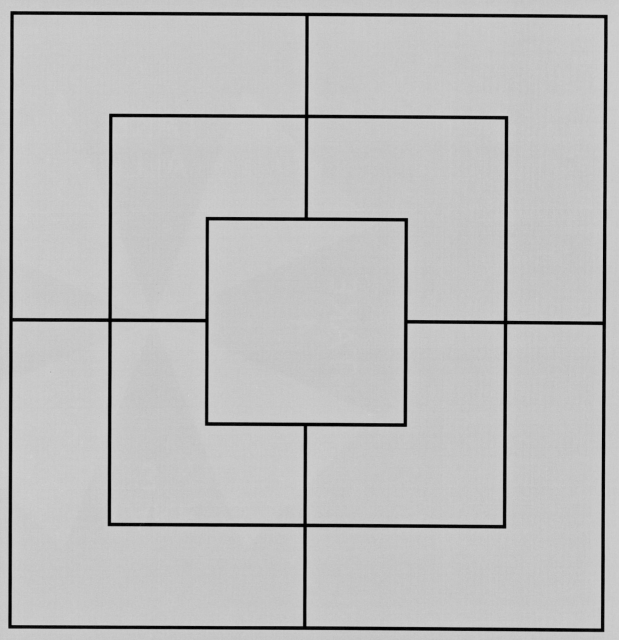

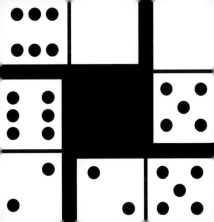

MAKE A
TRI-COLOUR STAR

Crease a sheet of card in half, and in one half, cut out a four-pointed star.

Fold the card together and trace the outline of the star on the other half. Then re-draw and cut out the second star so that its points are in between the points of the first star.

Place the cardboard on a table in front of a screen or white wall, and place two lighted candles of the same height behind it. The light will throw two shadows onto the screen, forming a single star with eight points.

Hold a glass filled with red wine or coloured liquid behind one of the stars and watch the transformation.

LAM TURKI

The object of the game is to
get nine counters on and off
the board in a certain
sequence.

Put the first counter on
any point, calling 'one'. Move
it in a straight line to another
point, 'two', and then a third
point, 'three'. Repeat this
one-two-three sequence for
each counter until all of them
are on the board. The first and
third points must be empty
each time, although the
second one can be occupied.

To get the counters off the
board, lift a counter over
another onto an empty point
beyond and remove the
intervening piece. In a series
of similar short leaps, remove
all the counters but one from
the board.

PICTURE CONSEQUENCES

This game is for between two and four players. First fold a piece of paper into four equal sections.

One player secretly draws a head with the start of a neck and then folds the paper so that only a small section of neck can be seen. The next player then draws the top half of a body with arms, and folds the paper so that only a small section of a waist can be seen. The following player draws from the waist to the knees and again folds the paper in the same way.

Players should try to be as inventive as possible. The last player draws the legs and feet, and then unfolds the paper to reveal often hilarious results.

THERE AND BACK

Write down a word and then change it into a completely different word in a series of steps. You may change only one letter at a time, and at each stage you must have a real word. The idea is to make the change in as few moves as possible.

RED
Bed
Bled
Fled
Flee
Flue
BLUE

COMPLEMENTARY COLOURS

Place two lighted candles in front of a screen or white wall. Place a figure cut out of cardboard, say a little devil, between them to produce two black shadows.

If a glass of red wine is placed in front of one candle, the shadow cast will change to red. The other shadow will seem to have disappeared, but if you look closely it will in fact have changed to pale green, the colour complementary to red.

If you use a glass of beer, one shadow will appear the yellow of the beer while the other will become violet. Substitute with a glass of water coloured with blue ink and make the other shadow orange. Experiment with different coloured liquids to see a variety of results.

Set out ten pieces for each player as below. The player's objective is to occupy the opponent's initial squares.

Pieces move diagonally one square at a time. If an adjacent square is occupied by an enemy piece, and the square beyond it is vacant, jump over the obstructing piece. The enemy piece however stays on the board. A piece cannot jump over its own colour.

At the end of the game, each player still has ten counters on the board, and the first player to occupy the opponent's initial squares is the winner.

FOUR IN A ROW

Draw the grid of six by seven
dots. The game is played
as fast as possible from the
bottom upwards.

The first player chooses a
dot on the bottom row and
marks it. The other player
then chooses one either on the
bottom row or directly above
the opponent's, and does
the same.

Each player continues to
mark a dot, playing upwards
and aiming to get four in a
row either horizontally,
vertically or diagonally, or
blocking his opponent from
doing so.

The winner is the first to
get four in a row.

LIFT A TUMBLER WITH AN OPEN HAND

Fill a glass almost full with water and place it on the table. Lay the palm of your hand over the mouth of the glass and bend your four fingers down almost at right angles. Resting your palm on the glass, raise your fingers and stretch out your hand. Lift your hand and the glass should remain attached to your palm. If not, try again with a different size glass until you can create a sufficient vacuum.

FIVESTONES
PECKS

Throw all five stones in the air
and catch them on the back of
your hand. Then throw them
up again to catch in your
palm. If you don't catch any,
start again. If you catch all
five, you can go on to play
'Bushels' on page 119.

    If you only catch a few,
keep all the stones caught and
with the same hand pick out
one between your forefinger
and thumb closing your hand
over the rest.

    Throw the one stone into
the air, pick up one stone from
the floor, manoeuvre it under
your closed fingers and then
catch the thrown stone with
the same hand. Repeat this
until you have all five stones.

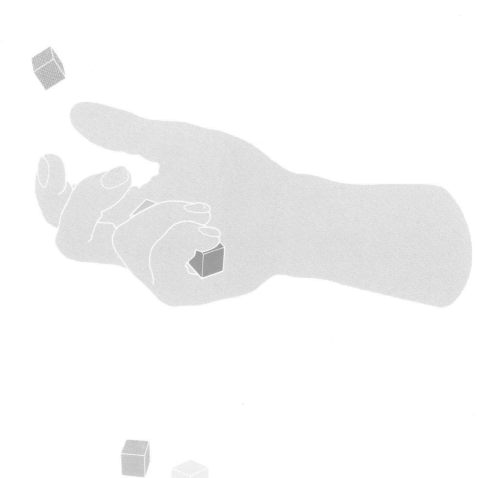

THE SLIPPER

1 Take a standard 30 inch (90 cm) napkin and fold it into four.

2 Fold on the red dotted lines.

3 Fold in to the centre.

4 Turn the napkin over. Then fold underneath and bring the folded section in front of the top portion.

5 Fold backwards along the dotted line.

6 Fold the corner down.

7 Tuck the point into the pleat.

8 Curl the top section downwards.

9 Open out the base and curl the 'toe' upwards.

10 A small dinner roll or piece of bread can be placed into the finished design.

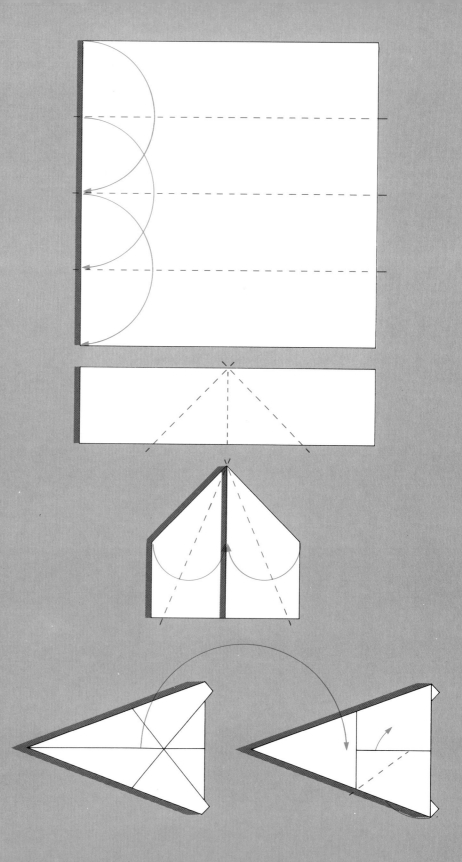

5

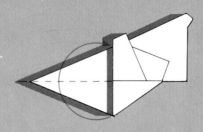

6

7

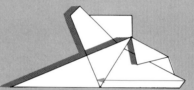

8

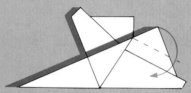

9

THE PYRAMID

Shuffle a pack of cards. Pick out the four Aces, and with the 15 uppermost cards form a pyramid, placing the four Aces two on either side.

If among these cards there are any which are in ascending order to any of the Aces, place them on the Ace of that suit. Fill up the blank spaces left in the pyramid from the remaining cards in the pack and continue to play.

The object is to build a complete suit on each Ace, finishing with the King. If you come to a standstill, you have lost.

NIM

This game should be played as fast as possible. Lay out any number of rows of matches forming a pyramid.

Each player in turn picks up any number of matches from any one of the rows. The winner is the player who picks up the last match.

For the next game, change the rules so that the player who forces his opponent to pick up the last match is the winner.

APACHE DOOR

For this you will need to start with the basic opening shown on page 9.

Convert the index loops into wrist loops by inserting the middle, ring and little fingers, followed by the thumbs, into the index loop from below. Let this loop slide down the wrist.

Combine the little finger and thumb loops by inserting the little fingers into the thumb loops and the thumbs into the little finger loops.

Bend the right hand down to grasp all the strings: draw them back between the left thumb and index finger, and round the thumb below the double thumb loop. Take hold of the double thumb loop, ease all of the strings off the thumb, and then replace just the double thumb loop. Now repeat for the right hand.

Slip the wrist loops up and over the fingers to lie across the strings, draw the hands apart, and the ornamental flap of an Apache tepee appears.

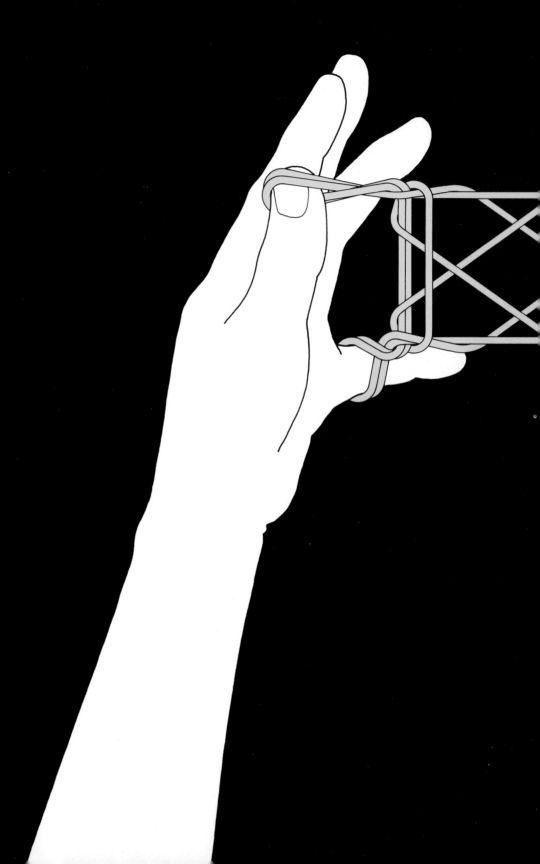

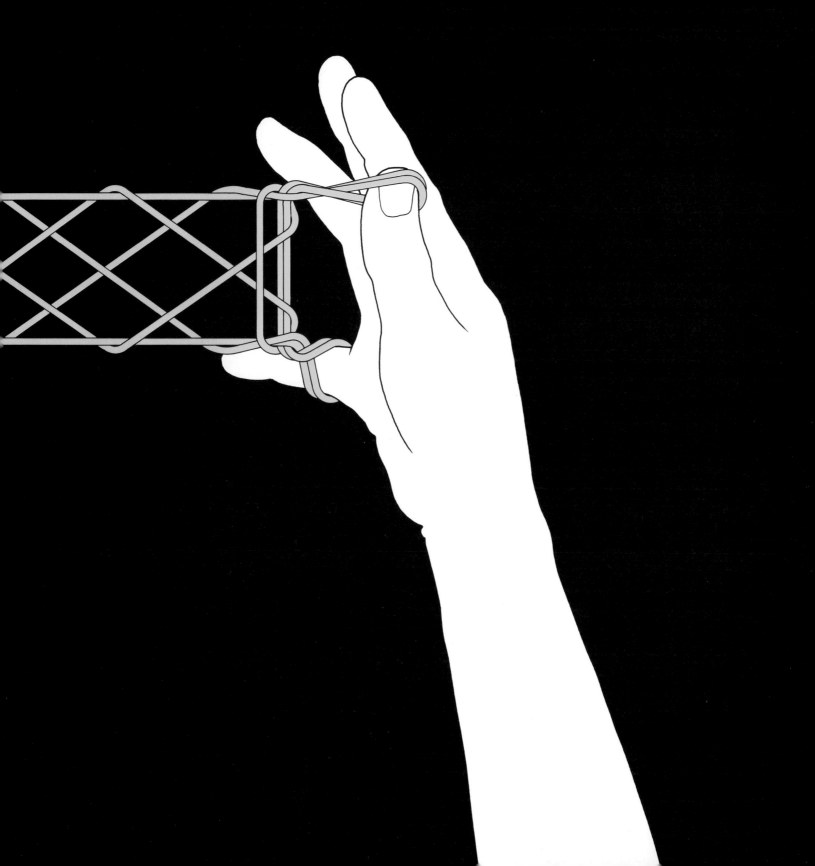

SOLITAIRE

Arrange 26 pieces on every
point of the board leaving the
centre point vacant. A piece
moves by jumping backwards,
forwards or sideways, not
diagonally, over another piece
which is then removed from
the board. The game should
end with just one piece in the
centre hole.

For a sample game, turn to
the solutions page.

hand is the winner.

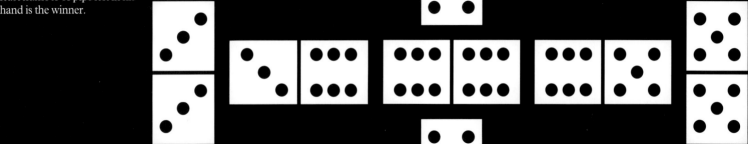

THE ROTATION OF THE GLOBE

Slightly moisten the rim of a plate with water, and with the yolk of an egg paint a golden-rayed sun in the centre of the plate.

Place half an empty egg-shell on the rim of the plate and, keeping the plate sloped and using a slight wrist movement, you can make the egg-shell revolve rapidly on its own axis while at the same time travelling round the plate. Keep turning the plate gradually round so that the egg-shell always has an inch or two (two to five cm) of plate rim in front of it.

This experiment illustrates the double movement of the earth, which revolves simultaneously round the sun and on its own axis.

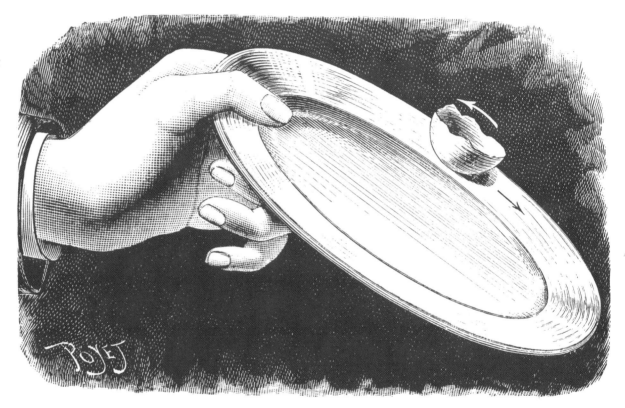

THE DIAL

Shuffle a pack of cards and choose any one suit, say diamonds, to play.

Turn over a card at a time, and whenever your chosen suit appears, place it in the position indicated by its value that corresponds to an hour marking on a clock face. For the purposes of this game, the Jack is 11 and the Queen 12, while the King is placed in the centre.

When you turn up a card of another suit, but of the same value as a diamond already in position, place it on the diamond. However, you can only place a red card on a black one and vice versa. For example, on the six of diamonds you can only lay the six of spades or clubs, not the six of hearts.

Any cards that can't be placed should be put in a pile which you can go through twice at the end of the first deal. The aim is to try and get four cards of the same value, red and black alternatively, on each of the 13 points of the dial.

SEEGA

Two players each have 12 counters, and open the game by placing two at a time on any two vacant squares except the central one. The objective is to capture all the opponent's counters.

Take it in turns to move a counter to any vacant adjacent square, including the central one, horizontally or vertically. If you trap an enemy counter between two of yours, remove it from the board. You may then continue moving the same counter as long as captures are made with it. More than one capture can also be made as below, where the white piece by moving onto the centre square captures three black pieces.

A counter on the centre square is safe from attack, even if it is trapped between two enemy counters, and a counter can move safely between two enemy counters.

If one player cannot move, the other must take an extra turn and make an opening for the blocked player.

CHAPTI LANGARI

This game is best played by three or four players. Stand at the start line and throw a stone into the bottom right square. On one foot, hop-kick it into each square round the circuit ending at the bottom left square. If the stone or your foot touches any line, you lose this turn.

If you complete the circuit, stand at the start and throw the stone to land just outside the top end of the grid. Then stand inside one of the star squares and reach for your stone. Step outside the grid, and with your back to the squares, throw the stone over your shoulder.

If the stone lands in a square, this square becomes your 'house' and you can chalk your name in it. The other players have to play round this square when it is their turn. If it lands in one of the star squares, or if you could not reach the stone in the first place, you forfeit the bonus.

For the next round, everyone takes it in turn to start on the second square, for the third round the third square, and so on. The game becomes more difficult as more squares become out of bounds.

After the final round, the houses are counted and the player with the most is the winner.

THE WORM

On a grid of ten by ten dots, the first player draws a horizontal or vertical line to join any two adjacent dots. The second player then draws another line, horizontally or vertically, connecting one end of the line to another adjacent dot. Players continue the game in turn, drawing a line from either end of the 'worm' to an adjacent dot.

The winner is the player who forces his opponent to draw a line which joins either end of the worm back on itself.

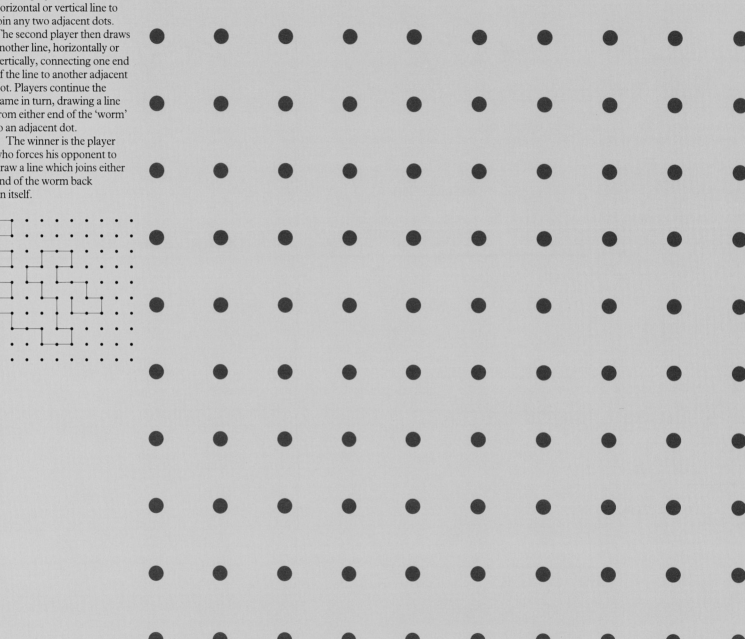

MATCHBOXES

Make the largest possible square using the matches from a large box. Two players take it in turn to remove one match or any two adjacent matches. The player who removes the last one is the winner.

PENTOMINOES

Make a pentominoes set with
the aid of the diagram below
using card or wood. The best
size is about four inches
(10 cm) wide. Lightly mark
the six by ten grid and then
carefully cut out the 12 pieces
of the set.

The game is to produce
silhouettes using any number
of the pieces without them
overlapping. Use all the pieces
to make a five by 12 rectangle,
a six by ten rectangle, a four
by 15 rectangle or a three by
20 rectangle, or try and make
the figures illustrated.

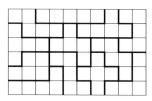

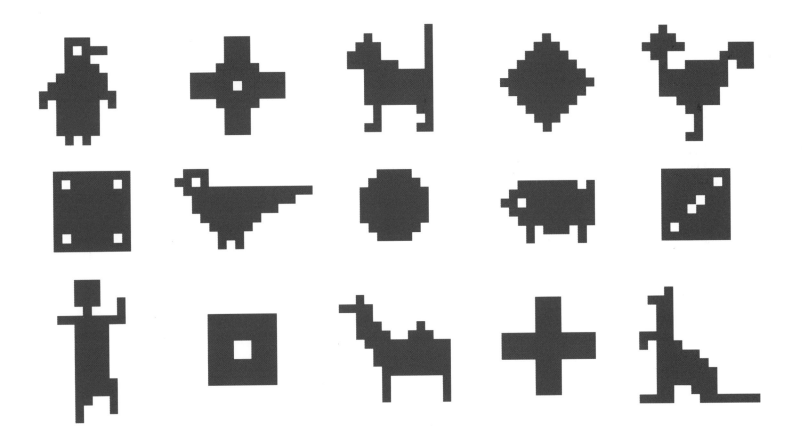

THE FLOATING AIRSHIP

Make your hands into fists,
stretch out your index fingers
and make the tips touch. Then
bring your hands up to about
eight inches (20 cm) in front
of your nose and look at the
place where they join.

Draw your fingers slightly
apart and look through the
gap, focusing on the far side of
the space in which you are
sitting. A floating 'airship' will
appear in front of your eyes.

REVERSI

Each player has 32 coins, one plays 'heads' and the other 'tails'. To open the game, each player in turn places a coin on any of the four centre squares.

Players then aim to place a coin on the board 'taking' an enemy coin as they go. A taking move consists of trapping one or more enemy coins between two of your own in any direction with no spaces in between. It may be possible in one move to take several coins in different lines simultaneously. The captured coins are not removed from the board or moved from their original squares, but turned over to transfer ownership.

The game ends when all 64 pieces have been played or when both players cannot move, and the player with the greater number of coins on the board is the winner.

WASTEPAPER BASKET

1 Take a large sheet of newspaper and leave it folded along its centre. With the folded edge on the right, fold it in half from the bottom to the top. Then open it out again.

2 Fold the paper from the top and the bottom to the centre line.

3 Turn the paper over from side to side. Then fold the top folded edge to the bottom.

4 Fold the paper in half from right to left.

5 Open the paper to form a right angle with the right-hand side standing vertically.

6 Keeping the left side flat on the table, open out the right side and squash the paper down, folding it to form a triangular shape.

7 Turn the paper over from left to right and make another triangular shape.

8 Fold up the bottom corners of the top layer so that the rest remain.

9 Open out the top layers of the paper and press it flat.

10 Turn the paper over from side to side and repeat steps 8 and 9.

11 Fold in the top layer of paper to meet the centre line, then turn the paper over from side to side and fold into the centre.

12 Turn the paper over from top to bottom.

13 Fold down the top two flaps, one forwards, one backwards. Then hold a flap in each hand and pull apart. Push the middle into shape.

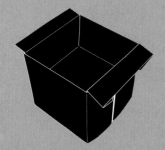

1

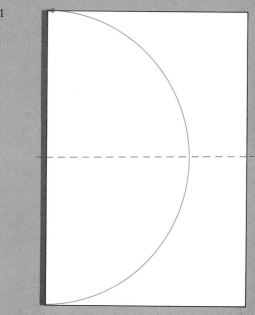

2

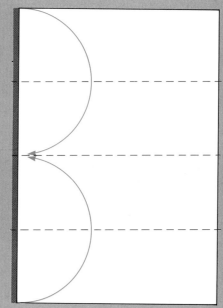

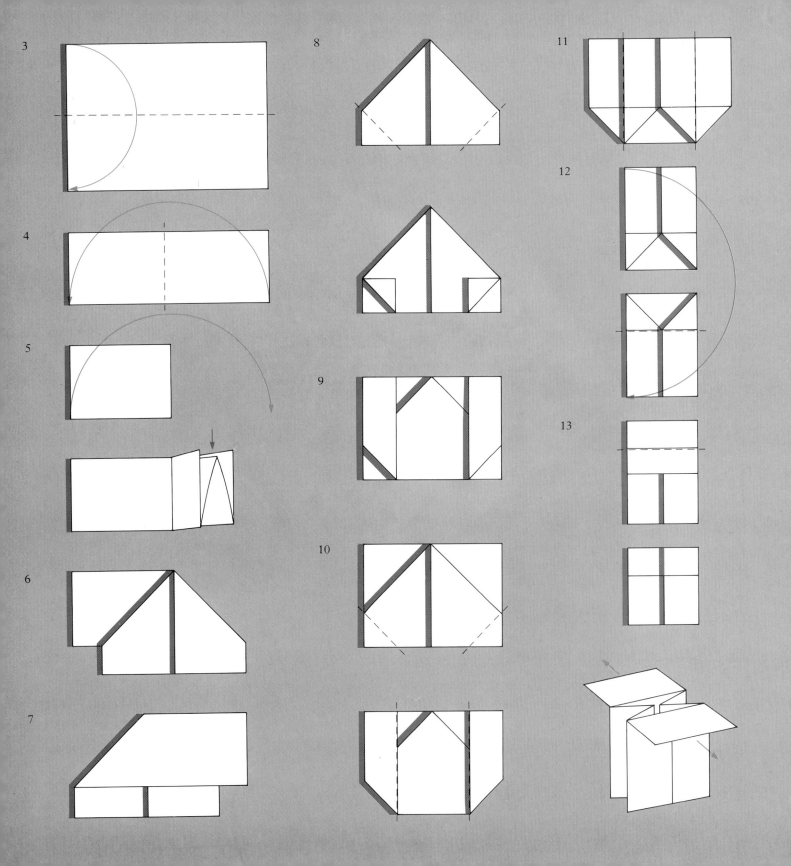

DARE DOLLOPS

Remove the face (picture) cards from a pack, shuffle the remainder and put them on the table.

Deal out the face cards, four for each player. Each player then secretly decides which face card to collect.

The dealer declares 'one, two, three, pass', so that on the word 'pass' each player discards an unwanted card to a player on the right.

This process continues until one person has four of the same. The winner then puts his hand over the cards on the table and the other players follow as quickly as possible. The last player to do so is given the top card.

Re-shuffle the face cards and start play again, until one player ends up with non-face cards adding up to 21 or more. This loser is then given a dare.

LAU KATI KATA

Two players each have six
counters which they set out on
the grid as below.

Take it in turns to move
one counter at a time to any
free adjacent point. If an
adjacent point is occupied by
an enemy counter and the
point beyond it free, the
enemy can be captured by
jumping over and removing it.

When possible, a series of
jumps is permitted and a
change of direction allowed.

If a counter can make a
capture it must do so, otherwise it may be removed by the
opponent as a bonus before
his next turn.

The winner is the player
who captures his opponent's
six counters.

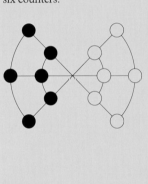

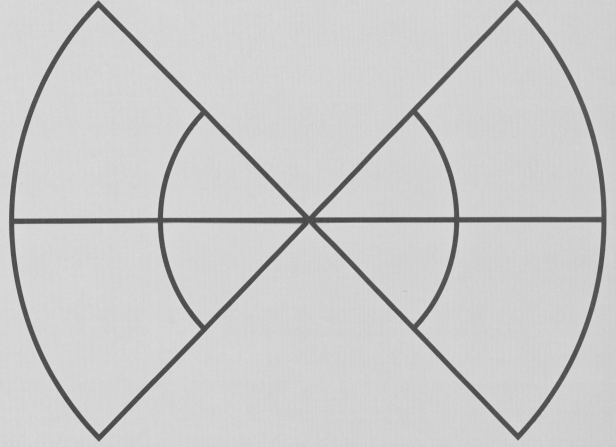

Two players each have five
counters and take it in turn to
place one of them on any of
the nine points of the grid.
The player who gets three in
a row in any direction is the
winner.

SEND-A-LETTER
HOPSCOTCH

Hop on both feet from square 1 through to square 9 and back again. Then hop on your right foot from 1 to 4, hop on both feet into 5 and 6 at the same time, hop to 7 on one foot, then on both feet to 8 and 9. Jump around so that your right foot is in 9 and your left foot in 8.

Hop once so that your legs are crossed, left foot in 9 and right foot in 8, then hop on one foot through 7 and 6, hop on both feet through 5 and 4 and hop on one foot back into square 1.

Hop from 1 to 9 and back again, hopping cross-legged into 5 and 6, one foot in each, and 8 and 9 in the same way.

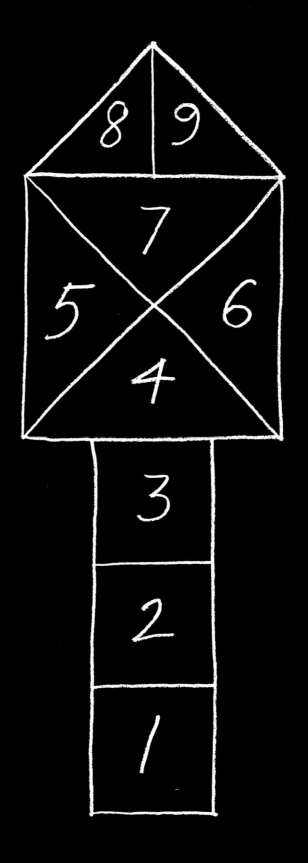

MAKE A COIN FALL
INTO A BOTTLE

Bend a wooden match in half
to break so that the two halves
are joined by just a few fibres.
Then place it folded across the
neck of a bottle and place a
small coin on top.

Dip your finger into a glass
of water, and holding it just
above the broken centre of the
match, let the water drip onto
the wood fibres. The water
will make the fibres swell and
the match will start to unbend,
until the opening becomes
too wide to support the coin
which will then fall into
the bottle.

ONE LINE NIM

Lay out 15 matches in a row.
Each player in turn picks up
one, two or three matches,
and the winner is the player
who forces his opponent to
pick up the last match.

AWITHLAKNANNAI

Two players each have 12 counters which they place on the grid as below.

Take it in turns to move one counter at a time to any free adjacent point. If an adjacent point is occupied by an enemy counter and the point beyond it free, the enemy can be captured by jumping over and removing it.

When possible, a series of jumps is permitted and a change of direction allowed. If a counter can make a capture it must do so, otherwise it may be removed by the opponent as a bonus before his next turn.

The winner is the player who captures his opponent's 12 counters.

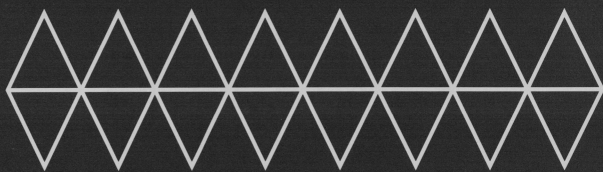

PAPER AIRPLANE 3

1 Fold a rectangular sheet of paper in half vertically and then open it out.

2 Turn the paper over, then fold in the top corners to almost meet the centre crease.

3 Fold in the side corners to almost meet the centre crease.

4 Fold in the sides to the same position, press them flat and then turn the paper over.

1
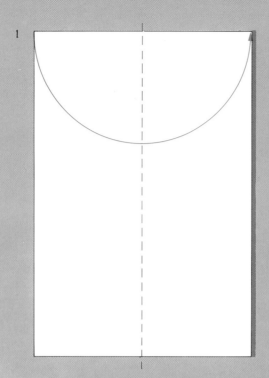

2
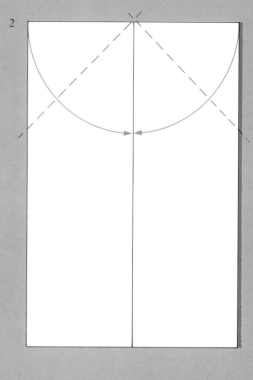

3
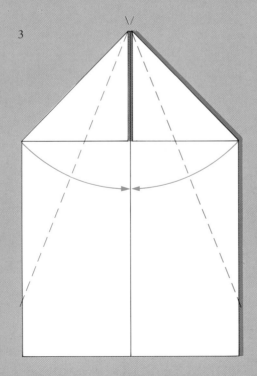

4
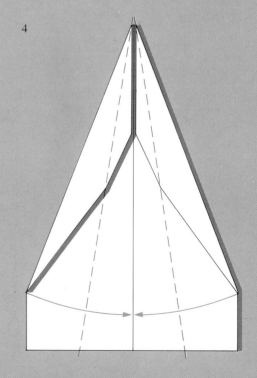

FIVESTONES
BUSHELS

Throw all five stones into the
air and catch them on the back
of your hand. Throw them
again to catch in your palm.
If you don't catch any, start
again, and if you catch all five,
you can go on to play 'Crabs'
on page 128.

If you only catch a few,
throw all the stones in your
hand up in the air and pick
one off the floor before
catching them all again in the
same hand. Repeat this until
all five stones are in your
throwing hand.

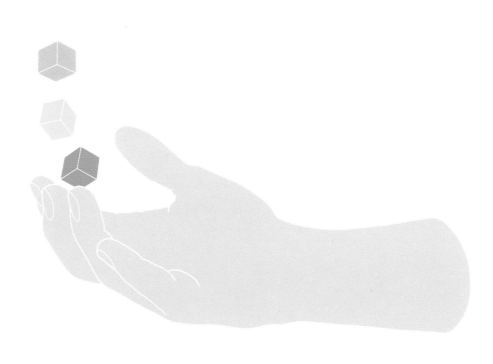

119

SHAPES

On a four by four grid, draw a shape in each square with any number of sides between one and six.

Two or more players take it in turns to throw a die and cover with one of their coins the shape whose sides correspond in number with the number thrown. If you throw a one, cover a circle as this has one side.

The first player to get three counters within a row of four in any direction is the winner. If there are many players, you need three adjacent counters in a row to win.

THE INDEFATIGABLE

Remove the four Aces from a pack of cards and place them in a horizontal row. Shuffle the remaining cards and deal them below the four Aces to form 12 piles of four cards each.

Once dealt, if a card shows that it is of the same suit and in ascending order to one of the Aces, a two to start, place it over the Ace. Continue the game in this fashion until you have four equal piles in order. If any of the cards in the 12 piles are of the same suit and in order to each other, place the smaller value card over the larger.

If you come to a standstill, pick up the 12 piles with the bottom right pile on top and deal them again with as many piles of four cards each as possible. This process can be repeated as often as necessary, but if you fail to place a card at all during one new deal, you have lost.

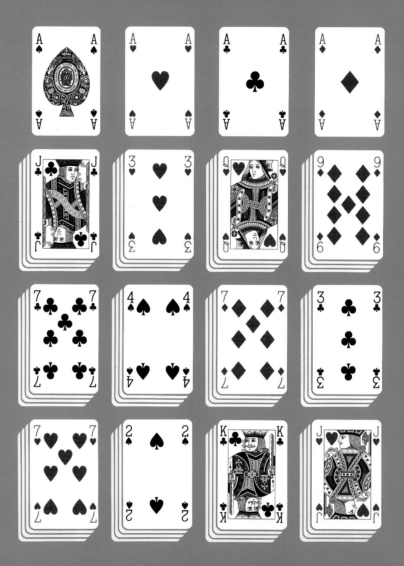

121

NOUGHTS AND CROSSES

This is a game for two players, one who draws noughts and the other who draws crosses.

Each player takes it in turn to make his mark on any of the nine vacant 'squares', aiming to get three in a row in any direction. The first player to do so is the winner.

CATCH THE JACK

Deal a pack of cards face down between two players.

Each player in turn quickly puts a card face up in a central pile. If someone plays a Jack, the first player to put his hand on it wins the pile. If by mistake a player puts a hand over another card, that card is handed over to the opponent.

Make sure you use one hand to turn a card, and the other to catch the Jack. The winner is the player who has won all the cards.

HINKEKAMP

Two players stand one either side of the centre line. The first player serves by balancing on one foot, and, with the same foot, kicking a stone into the other half.

Make your own rules for disqualification, for example allowed number of hops before a kick, heel kicking, touching the lines and so on.

The winner is the player who is strong enough to sustain his strength until the other gives up.

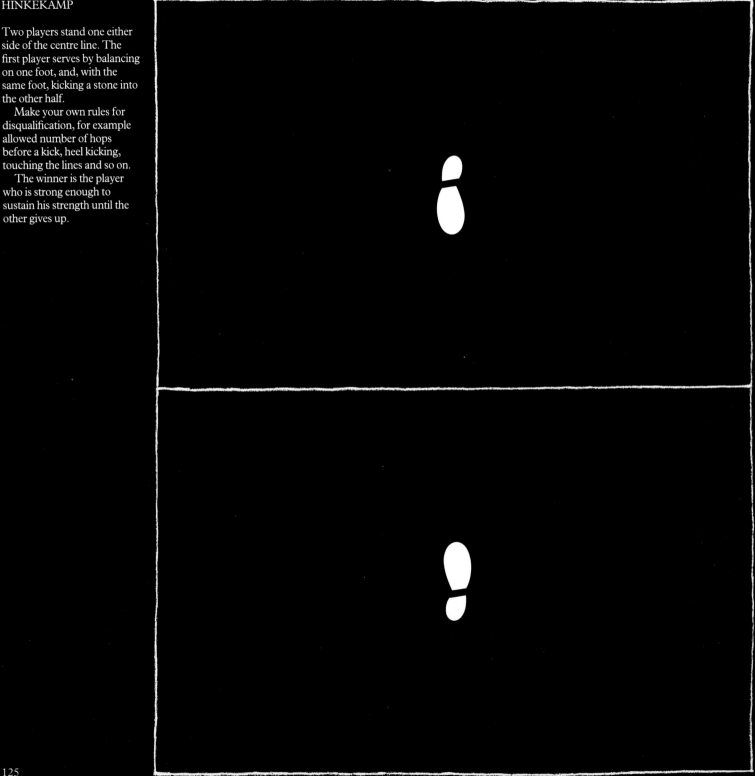

125

BATTLESHIPS

Both players each need two grids, one for a 'home fleet' and one for the 'enemy fleet'.

A fleet comprises six submarines, four destroyers, two cruisers and one battleship. A submarine occupies one square, destroyers two squares, cruisers three squares and a battleship four squares.

The players secretly mark their home fleet randomly, horizontally or vertically, using the initial letters of the ship type as below.

The first player chooses a square and calls out the grid number, for example 'E7'. If the second player has a ship on that square, the first player's shot will sink it. The second player must tell his enemy what has been lost, or declare the square blank by saying 'nothing'.

Both players take it in turn to fire shots, using their spare grids to map the enemy fleet. The battle continues until one player sinks a whole fleet.

	A	B	C	D	E	F	G	H	I	J
1					S			C	C	C
2										
3		B	B	B	B					
4									D	
5					S			D		
6		S								
7				C	C	C				
8										
9	S				I				S	
10				D	D					

HELP AN EGG TO DANCE

Boil an egg upright in a saucepan. Place the egg in the centre on the underside of a smooth tray, and place the tray over the edge of a table so that it can be grasped easily.

With your left-hand thumb and a right-hand finger at opposite ends, spin the tray horizontally, gradually increasing the speed.

Once the tray is spinning, the egg should rise on end and spin too. Grasp the tray, and try to keep the egg rotating by moving the tray in horizontal circles in the reverse direction from the way the egg is revolving.

FIVESTONES
CRABS

Throw all five stones in the air
and catch them on the back of
your hand. If you don't catch
any, start again. If you catch
all five throw them in the air
again and try to catch them in
your palm. If you catch them
all you can play 'Caves' on
page 142.

If you catch some but not
all on the back of your hand,
leave them there while you
pick up all the fallen stones
between the fingers of your
throwing hand, only one stone
between any two fingers.

Throw the stones from the
back of your hand and catch
them in your palm. Then
manoeuvre the stones
between your fingers into
your palm too without using
your other hand or dropping
any stones.

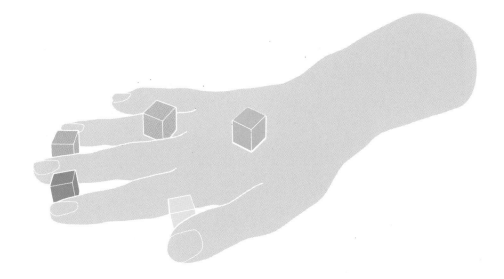

MOON HOPSCOTCH

Stand in 'Earth' and throw a stone into square 1. Hop to 1, kick the stone into 2, hop into 2 and kick to 3. Then hop to 3 and so on until you reach square 10. If on this last kick you miss 10 and the stone lands in Earth, you lose the game. If not, hop into 10 and kick home to Earth.

Neither the stone or the player must enter the 'Moon' area in square 6, with instant disqualification from the game if they do. Squares marked with a minus sign must be hopped on one foot, and those with a plus sign, on both feet.

5 +	6 (MOON)
4 −	7 −
3 −	8 −
2 +	9 +
1 −	10 −
EARTH	

ENNEAGRAMS

An enneagram is a word of nine letters arranged in a three by three square in such a way that you can discover it by moving from one square to another diagonally, across, and up or down, as below.

Challenge the other players within a set time to write down not only the enneagram but as many shorter words within the word as they can. All words should be from a recognised dictionary.

After the time limit, players score one point for every three-letter word they have made and one extra point for every additional letter in a word, therefore a five-letter word would score three points and a seven-letter word five points. If there is only the one nine-letter word to be found in the squares a total of five points is scored. The player with the highest number of points is the winner.

N	E	A
P	T	G
M	A	R

black square.

Players move alternately. The geese may only move diagonally forwards, one square at a time, keeping to the black squares. The fox also moves only one square at a time on the black squares but he may move diagonally forwards or diagonally backwards.

There is no jumping and capturing. The geese win if they block the fox so that he cannot move and the fox wins if he can break through the line of geese to the other end of the board.

BALANCE AN EGG ON THE NECK OF A BOTTLE

Hollow out the lower end of a cork slightly so that it sits on the larger end of an egg. Push two forks of equal weight into either side of the cork, then place the assembly on the rim of a bottle, holding it as upright as possible. After a couple of tries, you will find that the egg will balance on the bottle.

ENGLISH HOPSCOTCH

Throw the stone into square 1 and jump with both feet from 'Earth' directly to square 2. Hop into 3 on one foot, into 4 with legs crossed and into 5 with both legs straight and repeat this sequence until you get to 'Heaven'.

Turn round and go back the same way, pick up the marker in square 1 and hop over it to Earth. Then throw the stone into square 2 and so on, repeating the game in the same way for all ten squares.

While resting in Heaven you may stand on both feet. If your stone lands in the 'P' section of Heaven, you cannot speak or laugh during the game. If you do, you're out of the game for good. If your stone lands in the 'Hell' section of Heaven, you end your turn and must start again from the beginning when your turn comes round again.

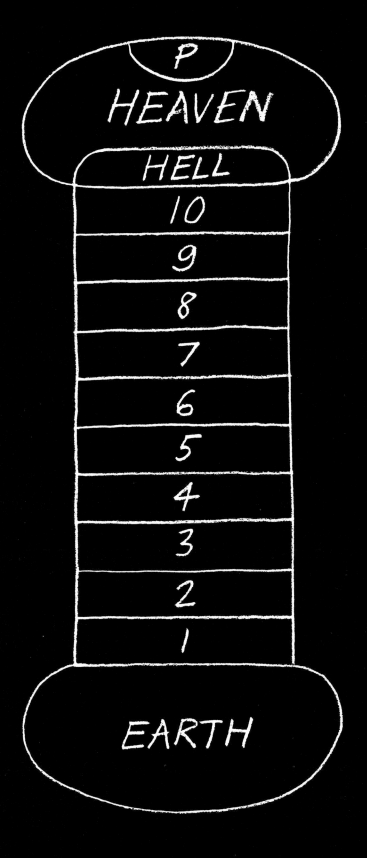

red, green, blue, yellow, to
finish at the centre square.
If you can't get there, see the
solutions page.

ODD OR EVEN

Place 15 matches in a row.
Each player in turn picks up
one, two or three matches.
Once they have all been
picked up, the winner is the
player with an even number
of matches in his hand.

THE ROSE

1 Take a standard 30 inch (90 cm) napkin and fold all four corners to the centre.

2 Repeat these folds twice.

3 Turn the napkin over onto the plain side.

4 Fold all four corners to the central point.

5 Hold a glass tumbler firmly in the middle of the napkin.

6 Pull the points away from underneath the napkin to form petal shapes.

7 Continue the process creating 12 petals in all.

8 A flower or small bouquet can be placed into the finished design.

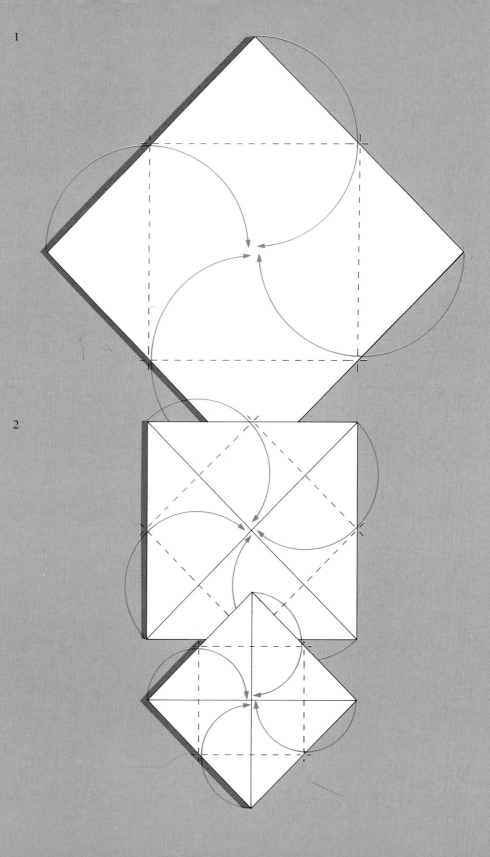

1

2

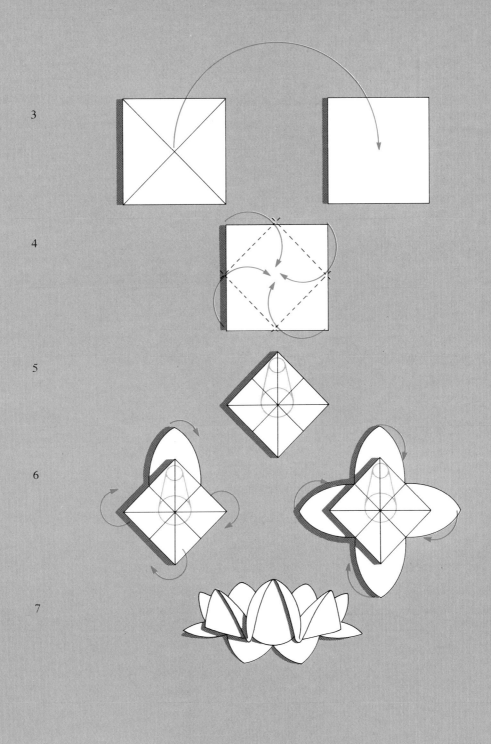

3

4

5

6

7

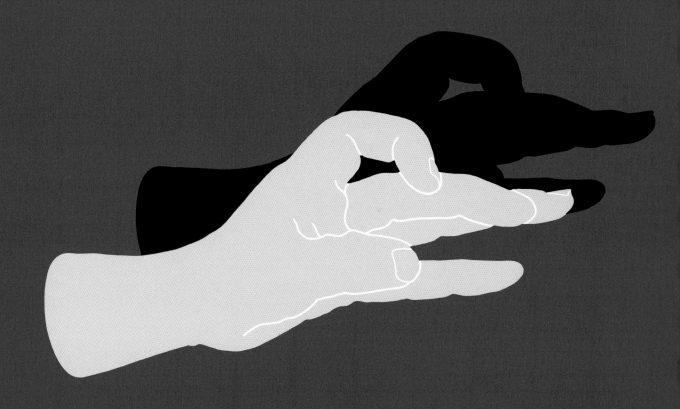

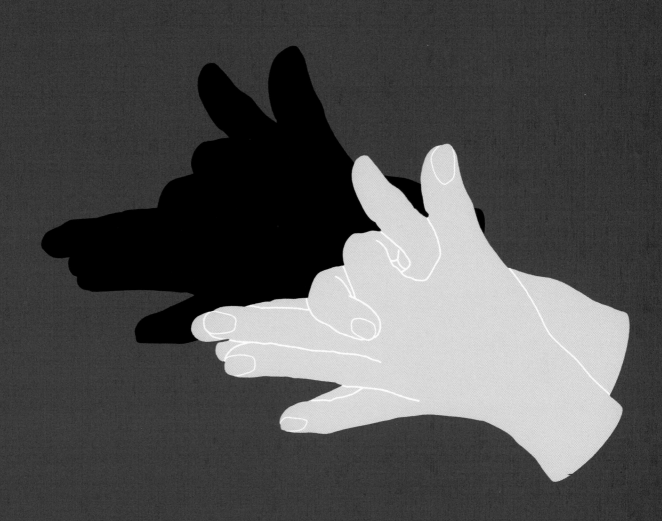

BASEBALL GLOVE

Take a sheet of newspaper and leave it folded along its centre.

1 With the folded edge to the right, fold it in half from right to left. Press it flat and unfold. Then fold in the top two corners to meet at the centre.

2 Fold over the right and left folded edges to lie along the centre folded line. Then turn the paper over from side to side.

3 Fold the bottom edges up, over and over, to make a band about two inches (5 cm) deep.

4 Fold in the ends of the band to touch the centre fold line.

5 Fold the top point down.

6 Bend the top down, tucking it over the points and underneath the bottom band.

7 Turn the paper over from side to side.

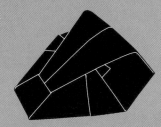

1

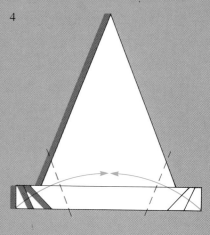

2

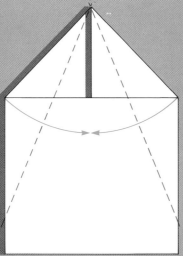

3

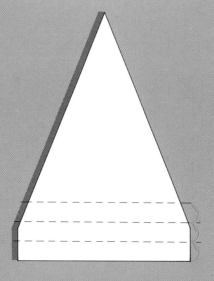

4

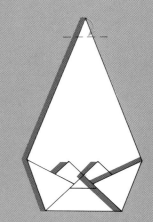

5

6

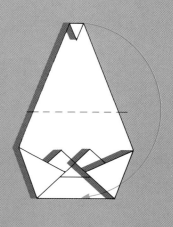

7

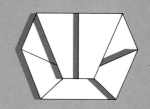

COWS AND LEOPARDS

One player has 24 'cows' and the other has two 'leopards'. The leopards try to kill the cows which try to surround the leopards.

The players take it in turns to place their animals on the grid, starting from one leopard on the central point. The leopards can move to any adjacent point, but the cows can only move to an adjacent point when all 24 are on the grid. A cow can be killed at any time by a leopard jumping over her onto a vacant point immediately beyond.

The game is won by the leopards if they kill eight cows, and by the cows if they manage to trap the leopards.

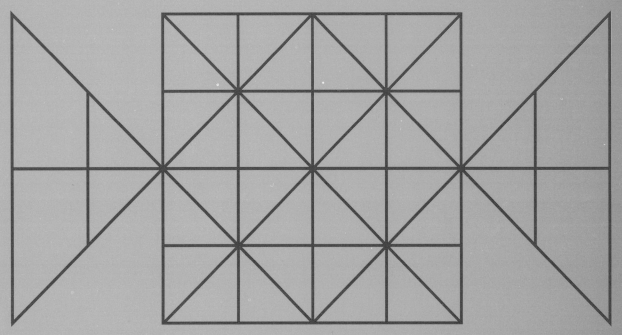

FIVESTONES
CAVES

Scatter the five stones on the floor or a table. Spread out the fingers and thumb of your non-throwing hand and place it near the stones so that your fingertips are touching the surface and your palm is raised. The spaces between your fingers represent the four 'caves'.

Throw one of the stones in the air. Before catching it again in the same hand you must knock one of the other stones into one of the caves. Repeat this four times to knock a stone into each cave in turn.

Move your non-throwing hand away, then throw the stone in the air once more and pick up the four stones in your throwing hand before catching the stone in the same hand.

Once you have played this game, go on to play 'Snake in the Grass' on page 156.

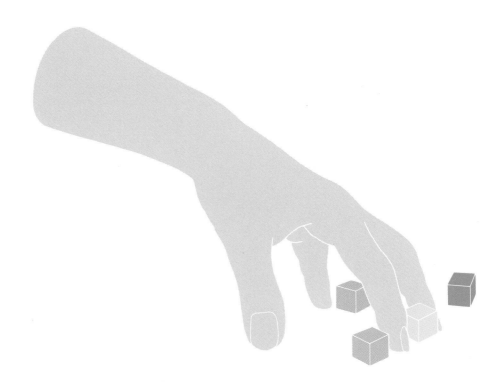

MAKE A COIN FLY OUT
OF A COVERED GLASS

Place a small coin in the
bottom of a conical glass and,
above it, a larger coin which is
a little smaller in diameter
than the glass.

    With the glass on a table,
blow hard on the nearest edge
of the large coin. This will
turn the coin on its own axis
and force the smaller coin to
jump out.

HOWLING MONKEY

Take a piece of string like the one on page 9, then place both hands in the string to make a wrist loop.

Take the near string and wind it around the left index finger and thumb in a figure-of-eight thus: back between them, round the index finger, back between them and round the thumb.

Do the same with the far string but around the left middle and little fingers: back between middle and ring fingers, round the middle finger, back between ring and little finger, and round the little finger.

Insert right index finger into left index loop and right middle finger into left middle finger loop. Draw the hands apart, and slip the wrist loop up and over the fingers and thumb of the left hand.

Place the tips of index and middle fingers of both hands together, transfer finger loops from right hand to left. Lift off the original left finger loops over the new loops, then transfer the new loops back to the right hand.

Draw the hands apart and the mouth of the baboon or howling monkey appears.

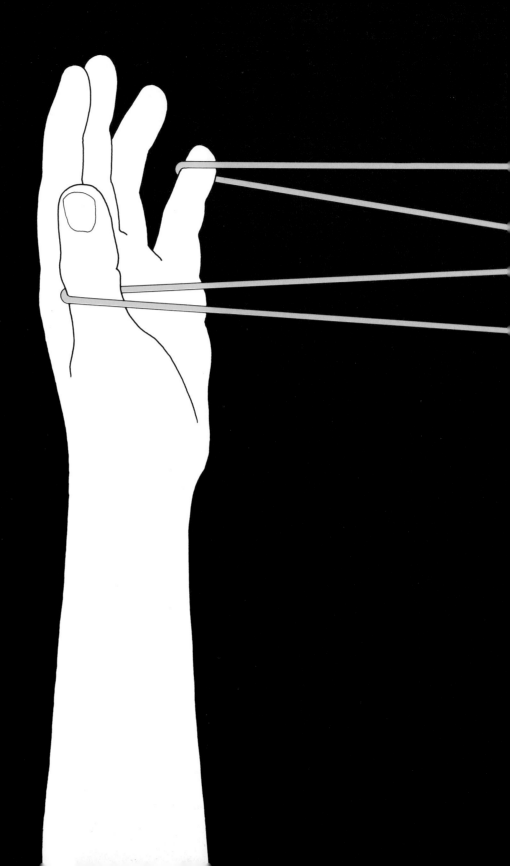

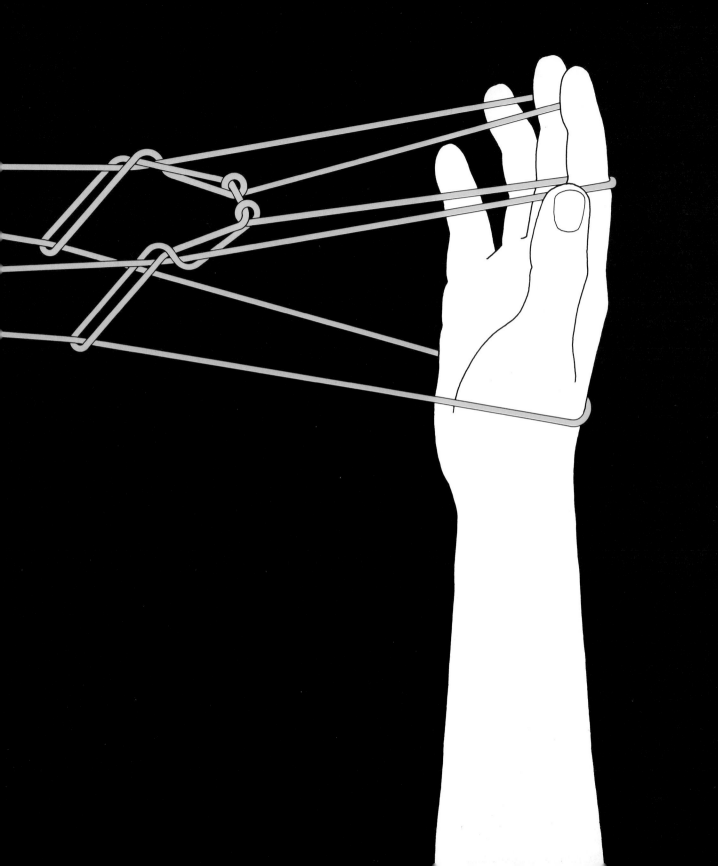

HIGH JUMP

Two players each have 12 counters set out as below. The object of the game is to capture or block the opponent's counters.

Take it in turns to move one square at a time in any direction except diagonally. Captures are not compulsory, but are made by jumping over an enemy piece in any straight line onto a vacant square immediately beyond. In one turn, a counter may capture several counters in a succession of short leaps.

The player who captures or blocks all his opponent's pieces is the winner.

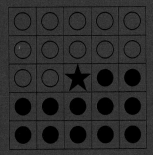

WATER HOPSCOTCH

Throw a stone into square 1. Hop into the square on one foot, pick up the stone and hop out. Now throw the stone into square 2, hop into 2 via 1, pick up the stone and hop back into 1 and out. Continue this way into each square and back again.

The 'Water' is forbidden territory in this game. If a player or his stone trespasses into the water, the game is over for that player. Blocks 3, 6 and 9 are rest areas.

After visiting all squares, the last step in this game is played without a stone: The player must hop on one leg three times around the whole diagram without resting.

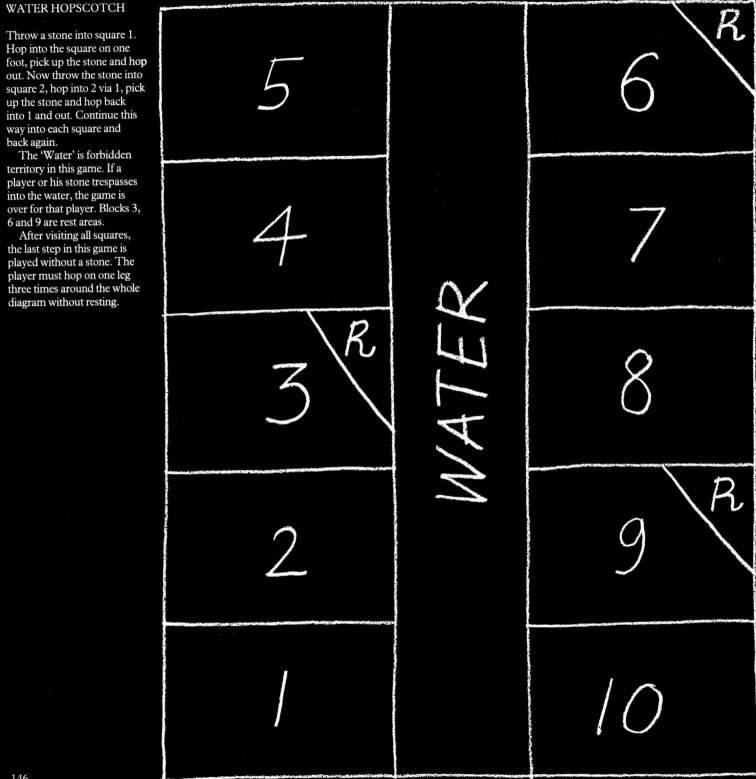

THE BOAR'S HEAD

1 Take a standard 30 inch (90 cm) napkin and fold it into three.

2 Fold the edges to the centre.

3 Turn down the corners to the centre line.

4 Turn the napkin over with the plain side uppermost.

5 Lightly fold along the dotted line.

6 Lightly fold again on the dotted line and tuck the corner into the pleat.

7 Form the napkin into a conical shape.

8 Place the napkin on the table with the tucked side forming the base.

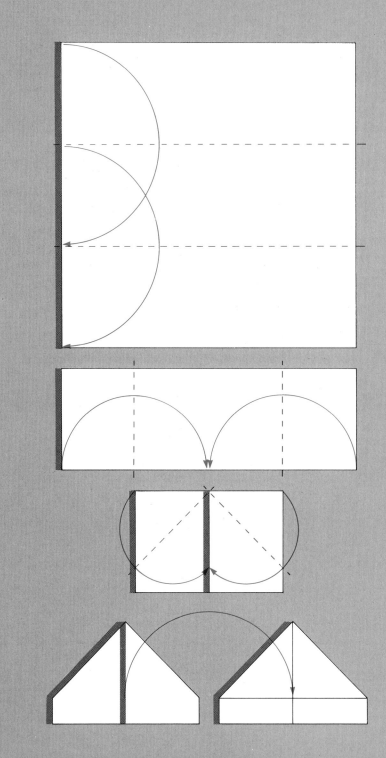

147

5

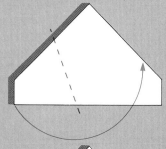

6

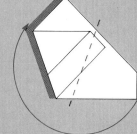

7

8

SHUT THE BOX

Two or more players in turn throw two dice and use nine counters to cover the numbers on the board.

If a player rolls 6 and 2, he either places a counter on the numbers 6 and 2 or adds them together and covers the number 8. The same player continues throwing again until no more numbers can be covered.

If the sum of the numbers left on the board is six or less, the player discards one of the dice and continues with the other until he cannot cover any more numbers. The board is then cleared and the dice are passed to the next player.

The sum of the numbers left uncovered is the players score. If all the numbers are covered during a player's turn, no points are scored.

When a player has accumulated 45 points or more, he is out, and the last player left in the game is the winner.

7	8	9
4	5	6
1	2	3

PAIRS

This is a game for two players or teams. One side takes the numbers 01234 and the other side 56789.

To score a point, spot two of your numbers together in sequence on a passing vehicle plate, for example 12. You can also score a point for a 'twin', for example 99. The first player to score five points is the winner.

GARDEN PATH

For this game you need two boxes of matches each with different coloured heads. Draw the diagram so that the sides of the squares are a little longer than the length of the matches.

Players in turn place their matches one at a time on any vacant line on the board. One player attempts to form a continuous line from 'North' to 'South', while the other tries to form a line from 'East' to 'West'. Each player tries to block his opponent by placing a match in the opponent's path while trying to complete his own path.

MAHARAJAH AND THE SEPOYS

One player takes one colour of Chess pieces and arranges them as below. These are the 'Sepoys'. The other player has a single Knight as the 'Maharajah' and places it on any other square.

All the pieces move as in Chess on page 24, but the Maharajah only has the moves of the Knight and the Queen. The object of the game is for the first player to checkmate the Maharajah while he tries to checkmate the King.

CAESAR

Lay out the nine cards and try to re-arrange them so that the number of 'pips' in a row, hearts, clubs, spades or diamonds, add up to 15 in all directions.

If you can't achieve this, see the solutions page.

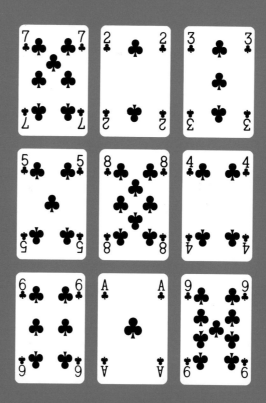

FOX AND GEESE

One player has one 'fox' and
the other 17 'geese' set out on
the board as below.

The fox in turn moves to an
adjacent point in any direction
and attempts to 'kill' the geese
by jumping over each victim
onto a vacant space. Multiple
jumps are allowed, and 'dead'
geese are removed from
the board.

The geese in turn only
move forwards or sideways.
Although they cannot jump
the fox, they try to corner him
so that he cannot move.

The fox wins the game if he
kills 12 geese.

TWO FIGHTING MEN

For this you will need quite
a stiff string. Start with the
basic opening on page 9.

Move the little fingers over
the index strings, pick up the
near thumb string and return
releasing the thumbs.

Move the thumbs under the
index strings, pick up the near
little finger strings and return,
releasing the little fingers.

Move the little fingers over
the index strings, pick up the
far thumb strings and return.

Insert both index fingers
into the central triangle from
underneath, and draw apart.
Lift off the single lower loops
from the index fingers over
the double upper loops.

Release the thumbs, draw
the figure tight and twist
the index loops several times
away from you before releasing them.

Insert the four fingers of
both hands into each little
finger loop and you will have
two 'fighting' men.

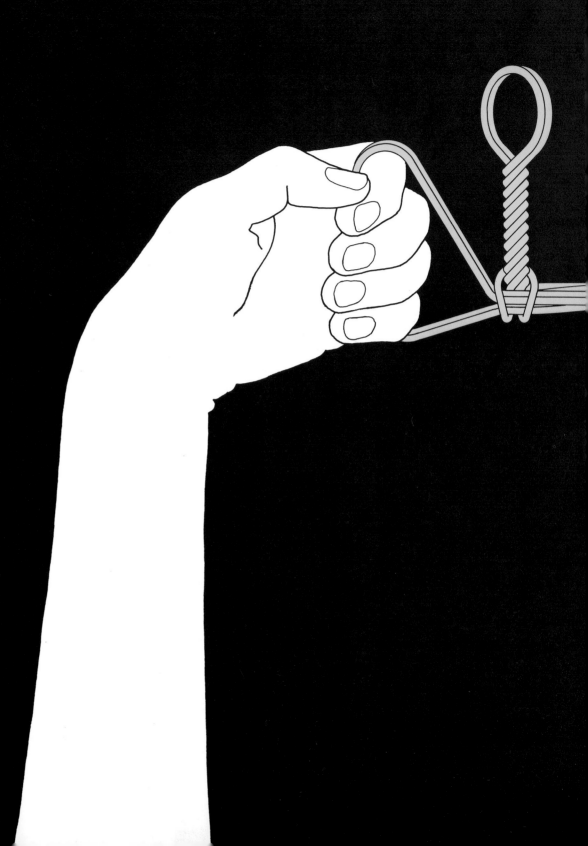

FOUR MOVES

Lay eight coins in a row with four 'heads' followed by four 'tails'. Moving two coins at a time, see if you can re-arrange the row so that every other coin shows heads. If you find this impossible, turn to the solutions page.

FIVESTONES
SNAKE IN THE GRASS

This is the final game in the sequence of fivestones, and the first player to complete it successfully is the winner.

Place four of the stones in a straight line about eight inches (20 cm) apart. Throw the fifth stone in the air and before catching it again in the same hand, move one of the end stones in a figure-of-eight movement around the other three stones and back to its starting point.

You can take as many throws as you like to complete the movement, provided that the stone is moved part of the way on each throw and you don't touch any of the other three stones.

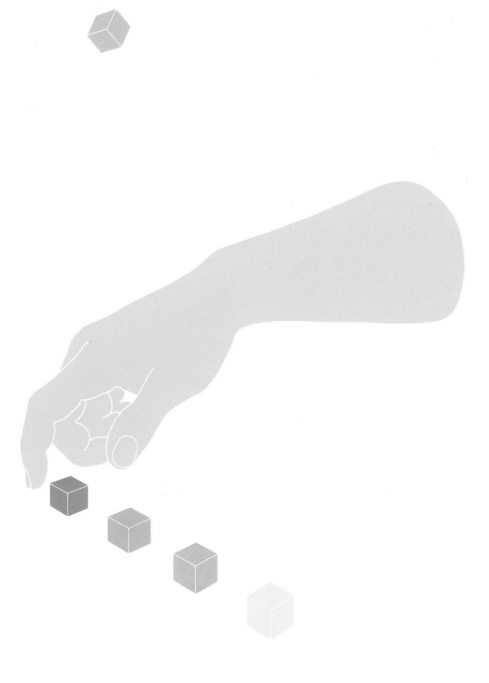

THE VASE

1 Take a standard 30 inch (90 cm) napkin and fold it into four.

2 Fold down the corners along the red dotted lines.

3 Fold down again to reach the perpendicular line.

4 Fold the right-hand portion upwards at the red dotted line.

5 Fold the left-hand portion upwards.

6 Fold the top left section forwards.

7 Fold the uppermost portion forwards.

8 Fold the top section backwards.

9 Fold by bringing the right-hand portion across, following the arrow.

10 The napkin stands upright on three points, producing two vase shapes.

11 A small dinner roll or piece of bread can be placed into the finished design.

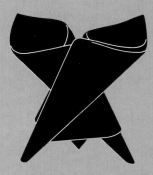

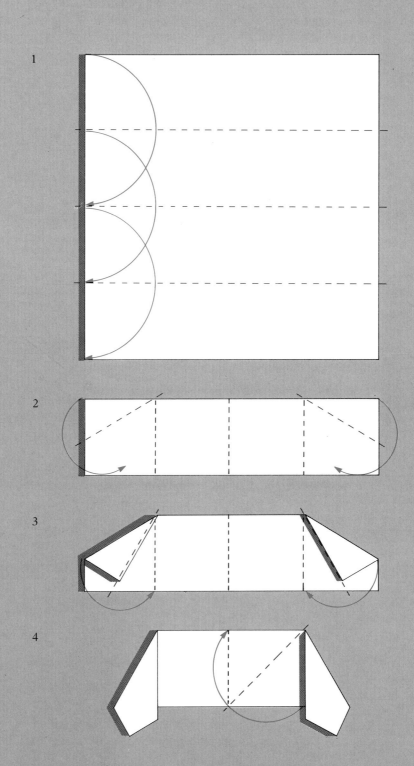

157

5

6

7

8

9

10

FIVE IN A ROW

This game is played by two or four people on a ten by ten grid. Each player chooses a distinctive shape, counter or colour and takes it in turn to place or mark one of them in a square.

The object of the game is to get five in a row in any direction, and the player with the most rows wins.

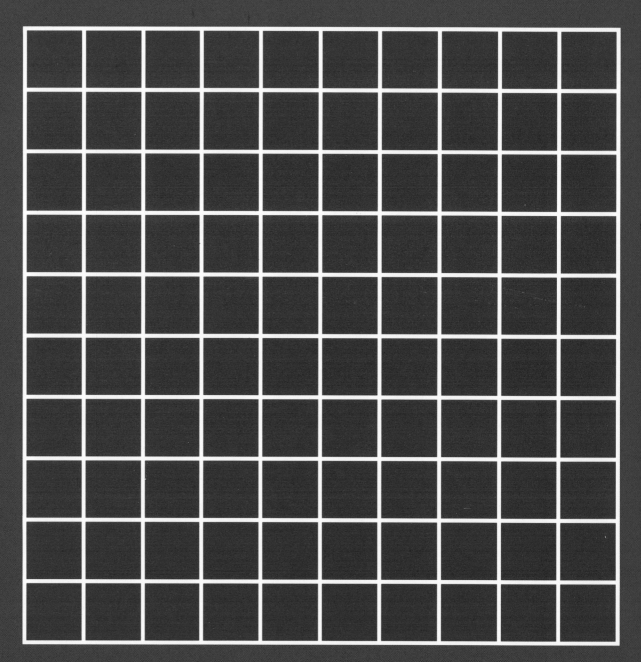

DOODLEBUG

Two players each draw the diagram on separate pieces of paper.

The first player secretly doodles a number between one and eight in the corner of his sheet. The second player then has to guess the number. If the guess is right, the number is written in the appropriate row of his diagram. If the guess is wrong, the first player writes the number on the appropriate row of his diagram and gets another turn. Continue in this fashion until one player has filled his diagram.

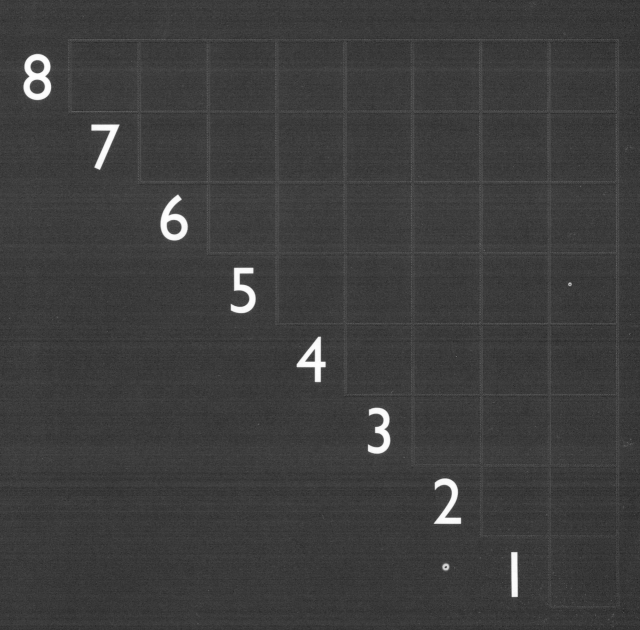

FLYER

This should be played as fast as possible. Place three sticks on the ground, starting with them about six inches (15 cm) apart. Players take it in turns to walk or run up to the sticks and jump over them, one at a time.

After each round move the sticks slightly apart and jump again. You must start each jump with both feet, and if you do so with one foot you lose your turn in the next round. The winner is the player who is strong enough to jump over the widest distance.

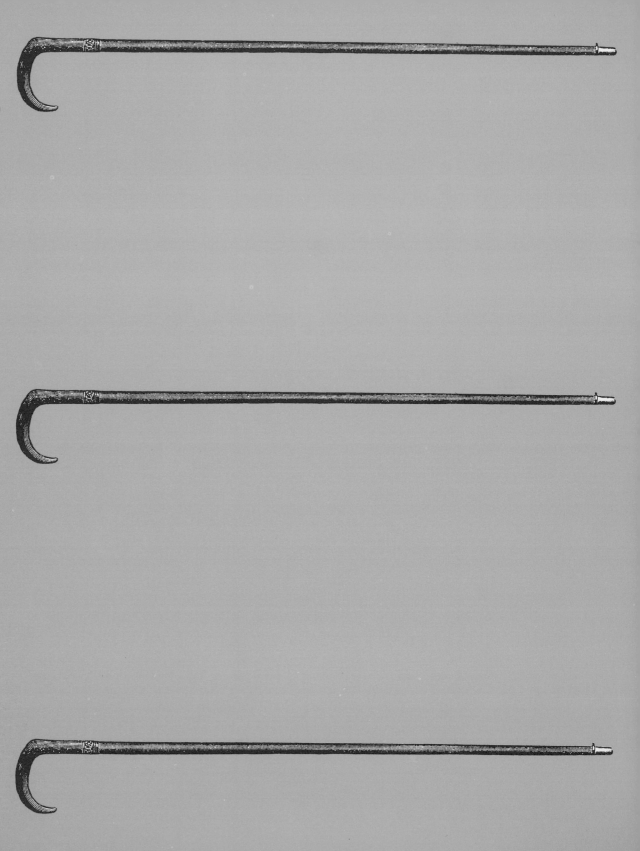

FOUR FIELD KONO

Two players each have eight counters set out as below.

The object of the game is to capture all the opponent's counters or to block them from moving. To make a capture, a counter has to jump over another one of the same colour and land directly on the opponent's one. The captured one is then removed from the board.

When a capture is not possible, a counter may only be moved along one of the lines one point at a time.

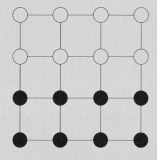

'heads' and the other 'tails'.

The players quickly take it in turns to place a coin on any vacant square, and aim to make as many rows of five coins in any direction as possible.

Change the game so that two coins of one player can be removed if they are caught between two enemy coins. For example, if there is a row comprising a head followed by two tails, another head can be placed on the other side of the tails which can then be removed. However, if a coin moves to make a pair between two enemy coins, nothing can be captured. No jumping is allowed.

Change the game again by playing on the intersections of the lines.

BACKWARD ALPHABET

With a group of players and a stop watch, take it in turns to recite the alphabet backwards. Anyone who skips or misses a letter is out, and the player who does it the quickest is the winner.

ZYX

Solutions

SEVEN ARCHES (15)

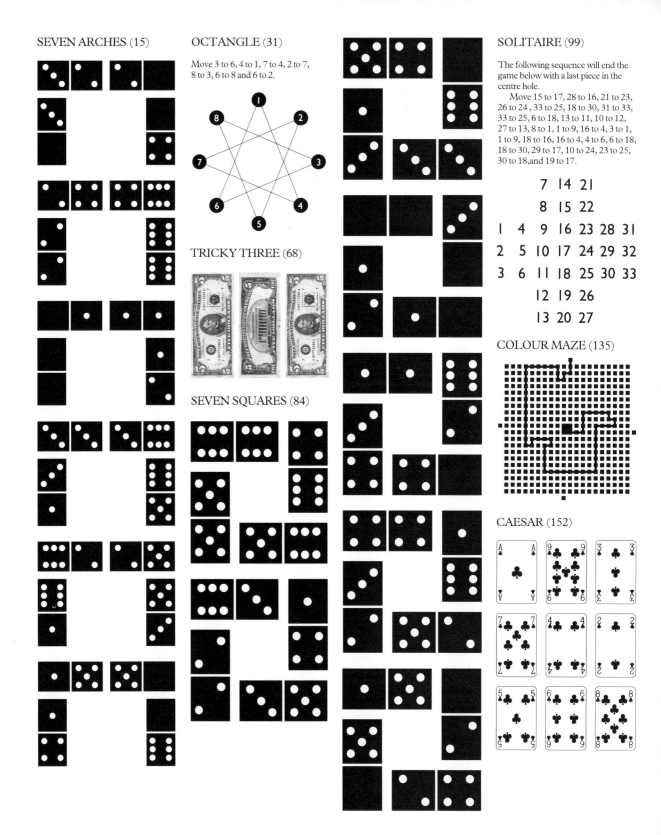

OCTANGLE (31)

Move 3 to 6, 4 to 1, 7 to 4, 2 to 7, 8 to 3, 6 to 8 and 6 to 2.

TRICKY THREE (68)

SEVEN SQUARES (84)

SOLITAIRE (99)

The following sequence will end the game below with a last piece in the centre hole.

Move 15 to 17, 28 to 16, 21 to 23, 26 to 24 , 33 to 25, 18 to 30, 31 to 33, 33 to 25, 6 to 18, 13 to 11, 10 to 12, 27 to 13, 8 to 1, 1 to 9, 16 to 4, 3 to 1, 1 to 9, 18 to 16, 16 to 4, 4 to 6, 6 to 18, 18 to 30, 29 to 17, 10 to 24, 23 to 25, 30 to 18, and 19 to 17.

```
        7  14 21
        8  15 22
1   4   9  16 23 28 31
2   5  10  17 24 29 32
3   6  11  18 25 30 33
       12  19 26
       13  20 27
```

COLOUR MAZE (135)

CAESAR (152)

FOUR MOVES (155)

Move 2 and 3 to the extreme end and fill the gap with 5 and 6. Then fill the new gap with 8 and 2, and finish with 1 and 5.

Acknowledgements

CARD GAMES
Cards reproduced with permission of Waddingtons Games Limited.

NAPKINS
These were inspired by Mrs Beeton to whom we are most grateful.

AIRPLANES
From 12,000 entries, these three won The Leonardo Trophy at the First International Airplane Competition.

PAPER AIRPLANE 1 (38)
Duration aloft winner: 10.2 seconds.
F J Hooven (professional),
Bloomfield Hills, Michigan.

PAPER AIRPLANE 2 (70)
Duration aloft winner: 9.9 seconds.
J A Brinkman (non-professional),
Dayton, Ohio.

PAPER AIRPLANE 3 (118)
Distance flown winner:
58 feet 2 inches (17.73 metres).
L W Schultz (non-professional),
Oak Brook, Illinois.

Pentagram is a design consultancy with
an international reputation in graphics,
architecture and product design. Since it began
as a five man partnership in 1972 it has grown
considerably. Today there are fourteen
partners, more than 120 staff and offices in
London, New York and San Francisco.
Their current clients include Reuters, Clarks,
Polaroid and IBM. Many of their designs
are household names, amongst them the
Parker 25 pen, the Inter-City 125 train and
The Guardian newspaper.

David Hillman, who has compiled and
designed PENTAGAMES, became a
Pentagram partner in 1978. He brought to the
consultancy considerable experience in
editorial design with the *Sunday Times, Nova*
magazine and the French *Le Matin de Paris*
newspaper already under his belt.
Editorial design continues to be his forte and
The Guardian and *New Statesman and Society*
are recent examples of his work.

David Hillman is also well known for his
non-editorial graphics, and D&AD awards for
the book *The English Sunrise* and his retail
design supplement the many awards he
has received.

PENTAGAMES is David Hillman's sequel to
Puzzlegrams, the book of classic puzzles.